Set Free

R. JAMES LOWN

WESTBOW
PRESS
A DIVISION OF THOMAS NELSON

WestBow Press books may be ordered through booksellers or by contacting:

WestBow Press
A Division of Thomas Nelson
1663 Liberty Drive
Bloomington, IN 47403
www.westbowpress.com
1-(866) 928-1240

ISBN: 978-1-4497-8171-2 (sc)
ISBN: 978-1-4497-8170-5 (e)
ISBN: 978-1-4497-8172-9 (hc)

Library of Congress Control Number: 2013900370

The author reserves the right to express his opinions and viewpoints in this book. The author
does not claim to be a professional therapist or have medical expertise. The author observes
life experiences with common sense and biblical understanding and shares his views.

Unless otherwise noted, the scriptures used in this book are taken from the New
International Version (NIV) for modern English understanding.

Some names have been changed to protect privacy.

Printed in the United States of America

WestBow Press rev. date: 1/10/2013

To my mother, whose love for serving others inspired me

In memory of my father, whose favorite song was "You Got to Stand for Something," the same way he brought me up

To my friend, Lisa E. Hartley, who described my writing as eloquent, the inspiration I needed to take action

I would like to acknowledge my team at Westbow press for their support and commitment in this my first writing project.

My gratitude to; Rebecca Romine, Brian Martindale, Amanda Parsons, Barbra Carter, and Michael Hyatt for leading an inspirational team!

Table of Contents

Introduction

Set Free is the good, the bad, and the beautiful of the Christian life. I wrote this book for believers and nonbelievers alike. Let's say a family member or friend invites you to church and you are listening to this strange but beautiful music that perhaps you never heard before. When the music is over, a man or woman steps up to the podium at the altar and begins to share a life lesson from the Bible. This person may give his or her testimony how he or she came to Christ, became saved souls, and received a life transformation healed from the broken life he or she lived.

You sit there and ask yourself, "What is this life transformation these believers talk about?"

You take a deep breath, stand up, and courageously make your way to the altar and receive Jesus Christ as your Lord and personal Savior. Right there at that very moment, something wonderful is taking place within you. The Lord begins to heal you first spiritually and then physically, and you now enter the process of personal transformation. This spiritual metamorphosis, comparable to the stages of the caterpillar to the butterfly, changes you from the inside out.

But it is a gradual change, not happening overnight. You are no longer the old person you used to be, suffering a life without joy. Sure, the pains of life are still there, but these pains no longer hold you prisoner. You are now a new creation in Christ. You attend church and read the Bible more. You pray more than ever for your family, friends, and nation. You even pray for people you don't get along with.

People who knew the old you see these changes, and they may not be happy with what they see. You have become a born-again Jesus freak, and you are no longer one of theirs. You are now one of those Holy Rollers.

"You have joined the illogical, Bible-believing land of myth and fantasy," is what some people who don't know God may tell you.

Once the people around you find out you have become a born-again believer, you may receive a chilly reception. Some may feel uncomfortable around you, as they don't understand this spiritual guidance you're speaking of. You have become a foreigner since receiving this faith and living a God-pleasing life.

Well, you are not alone. Not all people on Earth accepted Jesus Christ either. When I received Christ as my Savior, I did not understand anything about being personally transformed. I certainly did not take well to being treated like a foreigner because the people around me did not understand this heavenly understanding I developed and why I talked about God and Jesus Christ in my conversations. When you smile a lot, people think something is wrong with you, and I have walked with a smile ever since my transformation. Misery, grief, loneliness, or anger does not control me anymore, and that's why I smile. I'm set free. I'm no longer a prisoner, but not everybody understands this freedom through faith concept. So I invite you on this journey you are about to read of the good, the bad, and the beautiful in this walk of faith.

Chapter 1

Why This Direction?

As a young adult, I often wondered about the difference between religion and faith. Some people are religious; some are faithful. To me, religion appeared to be rules you followed to live a good life.

Take, for example, traffic laws. Will a speed limit sign make us travel at the regulated safe speed, or are we tempted to break the law and exceed the limit? Are we living a life of laws that we eventually break anyway, or are we living in a loving and conscious manner for the safety of our fellow human beings? We have a choice. We can obey rules and live in a safe society, or we can bend them and live in a risky, haphazard society.

What about personal transformation? Webster's dictionary defines transformation as "to change the condition nature or function." We have rules and regulations in society regarding proper and safe civil conduct. But do rules personally transform us, or do we find a way to bend or break them? Is life all about obeying rules and regulations, and if we obey these rules, will everything be okey-dokey?

The world around me was in constant change and still is. I would sit down and view the news, and usually the bad news outweighed the good. What do we do when bad news bombards? Good news transforms us, inspires us, and gives hope to a nation in uncertain and questionable times. Our people and our nation are in this desert of troubled times, and we need water. We need more than rules and regulations. We need personal transformation and a discovery of inspiration.

The year 2000 was a pivotal year for me. My father and grandparents were then deceased. A divorced man, I still longed to have a family and be a father. I had been in a relationship with a wonderful woman who treated me like a king. We were each other's companion. But we did not agree on one matter. I wanted to father just one child of my own loins. She already had two children and did not wish to have any more. I understood her reasons and honored them. My thoughts were heavily weighed about staying in this relationship despite the fact I would never have a child of my own. I painfully ended it with her. I was determined that fatherhood would still be a hope for me. I did not consider myself religious; however, at this turning point, I began to pray about this emptiness I had. The more I prayed, the more I wanted to know if this God of heaven, whom I had religion with, could help me.

I went Christmas shopping at the mall a week before Christmas. While shopping, I met a woman who captured my attention. I made conversation with her and asked for her phone number. I called her the next day and all through the week. We talked in volumes. In our many conversations, she expressed this joy and excitement in this church she had just started attending the year prior. At first, I was bit cautious because I was familiar with many news interviews that researched religions and cults. Truthfully, I was searching for some sort of spiritual change, but I didn't want to get involved with some cult either.

Back in the 1970s, a cult leader led his followers to their own deaths. I didn't want to be in a cult; nor did I want some dry religion leaving me parched in life. She described this church as personable and the leaders and the people as relatable. Because she spoke with such enthusiasm and her feminine charm won me over, I agreed to accompany her to this service of faith.

First, she invited me to Wednesday evening Bible study, but when I arrived from my home, I ran late. I walked into the quiet lobby and peeked through the glass pane of the sanctuary's double wooden door. I saw many people sitting in the row of benches with their head bowed in prayer. I did not see my friend. I didn't want to disturb the service either, so I waited patiently in the lobby. When the service ended, my friend came out. She was surprised I had arrived and introduced me to a few friends and people she had come to be acquainted with. They smiled at me and welcomed me to their family, as they put it. I liked them and decided I would come to Sunday service with my friend.

That frigid Sunday on a January morning in the Northeast, we rode to church together. We walked toward the lobby doors, and I observed this red brick building in the bright winter daylight. On the front exterior wall of the building extension where the classrooms were located, I noticed three crosses. I'm used to seeing a cross on a church, but I wondered what the meaning and significance of three crosses was.

I now set myself on an exploration of questions, hoping to get the right answers that would lead to truth. I was willing to listen to what these people had to say, form my own opinion, and make my own decision. I wanted rock-solid factual evidence before making my own conclusions.

I was at a spiritual crossroads. My inquiring mind wanted

R. James Lown

to know more about my friend's newfound faith since she mentioned they were a Christ-centered church (the first time I heard a church described like that) and they encouraged Bible study and daily devotion (also new to me). I would also hear that devotion time strengthens a believer's relationship with the Lord. I became extremely curious and set forth to examine these matters that were foreign to me. I had never heard of making my faith my lifestyle until I visited this church.

I entered the church lobby with my friend while also bringing a hint of cautious curiosity. The scene I witnessed in the large foyer was alive with excitement and people with candor. Greeters handed out church bulletins, and they wore smiles, the genuine kind that makes one's eyes crinkle. One woman greeted me and welcomed me to the house of the Lord. That was strange and unusual to me, but the atmosphere was inviting. We made our way into the warm sanctuary, and a relaxed and gracious atmosphere filled this spiritual house. The worship music was lively and triumphant. The organist released a divine harmony, and there was something about the rhythm that one just couldn't stand still and not be moved. Large screens, one to the left corner and the other to the right, displayed the words to the songs of praise.

This music was different. It stirred me, and now I was open to experience joy and truth in my life. Everyone in the sanctuary was standing, and most people responded to the worship music that inspired spiritual harmony by swaying or dancing. It had a strange effect on me. I wanted to sway to it. Actually, I wanted to dance, but I never danced in church before, so I just swayed.

Once the worship music had concluded, the senior pastor approached the podium to teach the Sunday message. He asked everyone to open their Bibles, so my friend and I shared one that the ushers handed out. He also suggested that everyone follow along in his or her own Bible.

He added, "How do you know if I'm telling you the truth if you're not reading it for yourself?"

Wow, I thought to myself. *I never heard that before in church!*

He began reading a scripture like a live story, a true account of ordinary, fallible men who simply followed God's will despite their faults. Suddenly I did not view the men of the Bible the same way as when I was a child. These men weren't perfect saints like the portraits of halos that you see. They were men reverent to God, but they were average, everyday men who allowed themselves to be available to the Lord's calling.

As the teaching progressed, the pastor encouraged the congregation to live our lives like Jesus did, no matter what setbacks we encountered in our walk.

This man, a humble servant of God, concluded that, when we go through our trials in life and remain committed to God, despite any failures we may have, it shows that our faith is no ordinary faith and our God is no ordinary God. His message was one of forgiveness, hope, and blessing, not condemnation and guilt.

I had never heard this kind of theology taught before, and for the first time, it made sense to me. His message did not sound rehearsed; nor did it condemn. However, his anointed words told the consequences of our sinful actions. His message ended with the truth that God is love and He wants to bless us.

I read further more in the Scripture, and the Word says that our God is love and his love overflows without end. He is the God of blessings, not curses! God curses sin, but He loves the sinner. He wants to restore us so sin no longer has control over us. Yes, we must repent of our sins and turn away from that which spiritually and physically poisons us.

To turn away, we must put our trust in Christ and allow Him to transform us from the inside out. When we allow ourselves to be available, His love is waiting to bless us, and we become blessings to others. When we walk in His love, we can love others. The definition of repent is "to feel sorry for an error, to regret one's actions, and to change one's mind." Repentance follows believing in the Word of God, the Bible. Once we believe the truths revealed in God's Word, we receive forgiveness of our actions against God and salvation through His only Son, Jesus Christ. Prepare yourself for the life transformation that will follow now that you have allowed Christ's spirit to reside in you.

The voice of the message came from the pastor, but the words, I believe, came from the anointing of God. I became sensitive to this strong, spiritual passionate love for humanity in this house on that Sunday morning. Once the service was over, the pastor opened the altar for prayer and anointing of oil. I watched people walk up the aisle. Some knelt at the altar in prayer, while others were standing, receiving hands-on prayer. Some people were in line to receive special fragrant oil dabbed on their forehead, a symbol of divine blessing. I made my way to the altar adorned with flowers and a table with an open Bible, a shiny, metallic cross, and a tablet of the Ten Commandments.

My friend introduced to me to Pastor Lou. He gave me a warm hug, shook my hand like a gentleman, and welcomed me to the church.

Then he asked me a question I had never been asked before. "Have you received Jesus Christ as your personal Savior?"

At that moment, my mind came to a halt. He and I were

face to face, and he got to right to the point. I knew nothing about this man, and yet beyond his rough exterior and tattooed arms, I sensed a changed ... no ... a transformed man. I knew I could trust him. An opportunity was before me, and I didn't want to pass it up this time.

In my spiritual deficiency, I confidently answered in a voice only those close to me could hear, "I am ready to receive Jesus Christ as my Lord and Savior."

He gave me another brotherly hug. "Welcome to God's family."

My experience at this moment is so difficult to put in words. I could not see God there, but He was there, working through Pastor Lou. I cannot see my own heart, but I know I have one. I can feel it beating. That's the best way to describe it. I could feel God's heart beating right there as though my heart and my heavenly Father's heart became one. Despite my faults and failures, I was received and accepted into the kingdom of heaven.

There is a difference between God's and people's acceptance. God accepts us the way we are, and He will make the proper changes in us for His glory and our benefit if we allow Him to. When we strive for people's acceptance, it is often at a price, and we lose who we are for someone else's selfish gain.

I connected with my new brother in Christ, a retired police officer born in the city and transplanted in the country. This man of Italian heritage who spoke with a heavy Brooklyn accent had a contagious ecclesiastical energy. He shared with me that, when he was among his colleagues and friends, he was a regular guy, although his faith had cleaned his former worldly mind and profane mouth. Myself being a volunteer firefighter at the time, I shared a common bond with my officer friend in

Christ, both of us servants to our community. He told of his struggles when his fellow officers discovered he was a born-again Christian. They often teased and questioned him about his faith; however, he continued to follow Christ. And soon after, he was ordained a pastor.

Pastor Lou prepared me with his encouraging words. When I am teased for this lifestyle of faith in Christ that I have chosen to live, let nothing or no one draw me away from my Savior.

What happened to me at this point in my life that I was willing to accept Jesus and become one of those Bible-toting, born-again Christians? I was living a normal life according to my society's standards. So why did I decide to become a Jesus freak now?

I was a child in the 1970s, and I was aware of these people called born-again Christians. Their ways of religion seemed abnormal in my youthful understanding. These people carried their own Bibles everywhere they went, and they spoke in tongues, which I had no idea what that meant at the time. They raised their hands up in worship to the Lord, and some even danced in the aisles. I witnessed a group of these people who visited my family's church one summer. This behavior that seemed especially crazy was unusual compared to our church.

Our service was much different. The music had a somber tone with the organ bellowing its haunting, echoed sound throughout the hallowed hall. It did not appear to move one's spirit. The service had a funeral tone to it. We sat in these uncomfortable chairs as I listened to a rather dry-sounding message. I would look around from time to time in boredom and then be amused at some people who had focused their attention elsewhere. Quite a few elder gentleman would be snoring until their embarrassed and annoyed spouse used an elbow to jab them in the ribs. A lengthy, monotone sermon usually caused this church nap. The message rested with some people in the holy hall but not everybody.

When the music service concluded, the minister approached his podium and began with a reading from the Bible. The message was usually on doing good deeds, and then we would come back the following Sunday and hear more sermons about God, Jesus, and the saints in the Bible and more on doing good works.

My mother taught me about Jesus Christ and what He did as a teacher and healer and how he saved us from our sins. For some reason, this message from my mother settled deeper upon me than it did when I heard it in church, where it seemed dull and rehearsed.

When I look back in retrospect, the message my mother presented to me came to life when she sat down with me one evening. She spoke to me in her soft, nurturing tone about a man so passionate for us that He gave His own life so we would not have to pay the penalty for our sins. She explained the good news of what Christ did so I did not have to be separated from God because of my selfish choices, what the Bible calls "sin."

Her message was very different from the salvation through good works message at church. My mother was my only spiritual influence, and being a boy, I looked up to the men in my life. I don't recall anyone from church sharing or discussing the morning message. In fact, most of the churchgoers were quiet about the service as if they did their Sunday obligation and then went on with their own lives.

I mentioned before about the movement I witnessed back in the 1970s when our church had interacted with a Pentecostal church during the summer. These people brought their music worship team, and when the music began, these born agains, as I heard them called, raised their hands and shouted, "Praise the Lord for He is worthy!" along with loud shouts of "Hallelujah."

"What was all of this about?" I asked myself.

Some were dancing their feet light and free, not in shackles. I did not understand why these folks were acting in such a way at a church service. Some adults in my life back then did not receive these people well. My father was quiet about his faith. I believe he was in conflict. My mother told me years later that one of those "saved" gentleman had a talk with him. She believes he was moved but remained quiet about it. I knew the men around him, his comrades, and if he claimed to be born again, they would have mocked him and possibly alienated him. I knew some of these men and heard many strong opinions from their conversations, and they were more resistive when the topic was about these Bible-reading, preaching, born-again Christians. I would hear these discussions about those Holy Rollers, and I was convinced that I did not want to follow them for fear I would be alienated.

I was already alienated in school for being skinny, nerdy-looking, and not good at any sports. Other comments suggested that anyone who followed a Bible-toting weirdo was not normal and must be in some sort of cult. So I chose to turn away from these people and ignore their life-changing message, as they called it.

My adult years were upon me, and my life plan was in my hands. From those years of attending church, I learned I was a good person and, as long as I performed good works, qualified for heaven. I also served my community so I would have no problem entering the pearly gates when my earthly time expired. However, I had many questions about life and uncertainties.

My family sat down and watched television news broadcasts, and there were always wars and talks of wars. Then in my twenties, the Gulf War broke out, and my fears and uncertainties grew. I thought about the government placing the draft into action if the war escalated and what would happen if I were drafted. Questions about life that church never discussed flooded my mind. Is heaven real? Is there a real hell? Is there life after death? Dying for my country was not a fear after all. I was a volunteer firefighter, but war would make death a close reality. And where would my soul go if I died? Could I be sure that I would go to heaven?

The church never secured that question for me. Those church messages were always about people doing good deeds to get to heaven, but I knew my intentions, and they weren't all that good honestly. I was a very selfish person. All my actions had some sort of motive to get a reward. Rarely did I do something out of genuine generosity. As long as I was alive, I was okay, but I wasn't prepared for death.

Although I heard a pearly gates description about heaven, I had pretty much brushed off hell. The church never brought these life issues to deep discussion. The way the church presented the message, a person's good deeds qualified his or her soul for heaven. That was how I interpreted the message anyway. I didn't want to just qualify for heaven; I wanted to be certain that my name was in the Book of Life. I had so many questions, and the answers I did receive were obscure.

I also gave into many superstitions and believed tales of woe and bad luck. I was once on vacation on the East Coast with some friends and visited a lighthouse with an unusual archway that resembled some type of dinosaur bone structure. Whatever it was, it looked creepy, so I went around it. One of my friends told me that the local legend of this strange arch structure warned of bad luck if one did not go through it, but I still walked around it.

I eventually learned that my own lack of wisdom caused the bad luck in my life and I had no spiritual grounding as reinforcement. I would pick up found coins on the ground that were heads up only, and then I would count this find as good luck. (I now acknowledge coins I find on the ground as a blessing. After all, God's name is on our currency.)

My life did not go as planned while I was at the control panel, so I would make many immature and self-centered decisions, some of which were directed toward my own pleasure and convenience. I had given myself a timeline. I would be married by twenty-five. (I was in my mid-twenties when I married my first wife.) Then I would have a house and children by my thirties. But I had no clue on the meaning of marriage or the vows. I knew marriage only as a tradition. My only blueprint available was the secular marriages of other couples I knew who did not live by biblical principles of marriage.

My ignorance and immaturity regarding relationships and commitment caused our marriage to fail. I also had a drinking problem. I often skipped out on my wife many nights to get intoxicated with a few friends. One night out of several, some friends would drop me off, inebriated, on a Friday night. I would see the silhouette of my lonely wife in the bedroom window, waiting for her delinquent husband to arrive home. Our marriage lasted only a few years and eventually disintegrated. I treated marriage like a tradition or rite of passage, not an institution of sacrificial love and companionship.

Some time went by, and I began to think about going back to church and giving it a chance to work in my life. I thought about giving my religion another opportunity to change my life because church was about family and I longed for that. I hadn't attended church since I started working in a grocery store, and I always worked Sunday mornings.

Maybe the church had some answers now that I was more mature to listen to the message. Deep down, I regretted my selfish actions toward other people, and a hunger grew in me for values and a commitment to have a family of my own and a quest for truth. I had many unanswered questions about life, faith, and my purpose here on Earth.

I started attending my old church once again. I stayed after service, got on my knees, and prayed so I could be closer to God and have a family one day. I wanted to read the Bible for myself, but it was not encouraged. I wanted to know more about God and find out if these were mere stories in the Bible or actual accounts of people who once lived. I also asked in prayer what heaven was like and if there were a real hell. The church mentioned hell on rare occasion but never studied the subject.

At this point, I came to a conclusion about hell. If the church didn't talk about it, then maybe the place wasn't so bad, if it existed at all. Other than church, I heard about hell in rock-and-roll songs, and it sounded like a big party place where all my friends would be. But the fact that the subject of hell was never discussed or studied in church only secured my belief that the place did not exist. My search for answers for answers continued, and I wondered where I would find this truth I was looking for.

I continued to pray night after night without ceasing for the truth about God, heaven, and a life of purpose. I wanted to know what the Bible had to say. Could it change my life? Was the Bible just stories like the fairy tales I heard in my childhood, or did it have true living accounts of men whom I could relate to?

When my new friend introduced me to this church, to my surprise, it was a Pentecostal church or, in plain English, a born-again church. (Jesus told Nicodemus in John 3:3, "I tell you the truth, no one can see the kingdom of God unless he is born again.") They were just the people I tried to avoid in my life. However, this time, I wasn't so quick to dismiss them. My hunger for truth and a life of purpose weakened my rebellion, along with a tendency for other people to misguide me.

Earlier, I described the worship music and the joy that people experienced through the power of this harmony to free one's soul of emptiness and despair. In the days and months to follow, I would listen to countless personal testimonies of men and woman who gave their hearts to Christ and who were healed of the pains and misery. They were abandoned, meaning they came from living a life separate from God. I listened and observed. No longer did I consider myself alone. For the first time, I received hope of spiritual truth that would not leave me in the darkness; nor would I be roaming in my personal desert thirsting.

Pastor Lou and the brothers from the church shared with me that walking by this would not be easy. I was about to go through the process of turning from earthly bound to heavenly bound. Instead of living my life against God, I was now living my life for Him. I was affectionately called a "baby" Christian, meaning I was growing in my newborn (new creation in Christ) life of faith. I had to learn how to walk in God's principles.

I repented and received Christ in my life. Now I was ready to grow spiritually mature one day at a time. I viewed life and my activities, specifically what I used to do for fun and selfish delight, differently. I now realized these actions were destructive to my mind, body, and soul, not only the other people in my life. When I thought about the mistakes and bad decisions of my past, my new family in faith comforted me in the counsel that, in the moment I received Christ as my Savior, the dirt and filth of my past was washed away.

Every day brings a pearl of wisdom that I have learned from reading the Bible. My life has been a gradual change in my new walk of faith, and I now use God's Word as my guiding light. The Bible can help you with many decisions in life, but you need to give it a chance. Wisdom and direction in life requires studying the Bible. Even though I accepted the Lord as my Savior, I made some unwise decisions.

I met this woman, and although we had a brief dating period, we talked about life, family matters, and a possible future together. At the time, we seemed to have congruency, and I shared with her my strong and urgent desire to be a father. She agreed that she wanted a family, and the prospect of having a child of my own flesh and blood canceled my wisdom to consider some important matters. Due to the brevity of our dating period, I failed to seal any compatibility or possibility of companionship between us. We had very contrasting personalities in various life issues. Perhaps we should have kept our relationship as purely platonic.

In my haste and lack of understanding, I expedited our friendship into marriage. This decision would cost me another failed marriage and the friendships of fellow congregants who chose to keep some distance from me because of my decision. When you go through a crisis, only you know your situation, and only you feel your pain. My spiritual infancy caused me to fail in observing our incompatibility of our personalities and viewpoints. Anger, bitterness, and disrespect replaced trust, honor, and respect.

There is nothing easy about ending a relationship, especially when a man desires that companionship to complete his life. Not all of us have had the opportunity of being raised in a Bible-versed, believing family or knowing personally what the Bible says about marriage and a man and woman's role in it. I had been through one divorce already.

Did I want to go through it again, knowing the pain and suffering it causes? Whether you are a husband or a wife making this decision, you are the only one who understands the anguish and torment you are dealing with.

I asked myself, "Is there any other way?"

The answer was no. We were wrong for each other. Had we courted, I truly believe we would have agreed to just stay friends. However, I did not understand the principles or reasons for a man to court a woman. I only understood dating and living together at the time. This act of marital dissolution prevented further hostility and emotional scars that could have become worse to the point of emotional and mental abuse. Staying together would have made us two enemies trapped in an extremely toxic relationship.

All through this family crisis, I prayed for our children and us. It is unfortunate that I could not maintain a relationship with my ex's son after the divorce. My desire was to keep brother and sister together on special outings. I do not advocate divorce unless the marriage involves physical abuse. In some situations where there is mental abuse, a spouse may need to remove himself or herself. Irreconcilable differences are not an excuse for divorce. You can work out these issues. You don't divorce your wife because she burned your dinner; you don't divorce your husband because he forgot to take out the garbage. However, physical and mental abuse is dangerous and damaging in a relationship.

Many believers kept their distance from me because of our situation. When this happened, my emotions had a stronghold on me. I felt betrayed by those who were supposed to stand up for their fellow believers. They were not walking in my shoes, and I began to build anger and forgiveness toward them. I had allowed resentment and selfish pity to cloud my mind for some time. Matter of fact, my angered emotions originally filled the pages I had written for this book.

After reading them over carefully, I asked myself, "Will these pity pages help anyone?"

A few days later, I thought about what I learned about my faith and why I chose this road. Somewhere, a believer is going or has gone through trials and crises in his or her life. Forgiveness, love, and hope is the basis of our faith, and Jesus promised us that we receive His love, hope, and forgiveness in Him. I have received the Lord's exoneration.

During this time, I recalled what Pastor Lou shared with me that turned around my ill thoughts and made me think about Jesus and His misguided apostles. My brother in Christ explained to me that there are no perfect Christians; nor are there any perfect churches.

He added this advice, "If someone thinks he or she has a perfect church, I'll join it, and it won't be perfect anymore."

I often thought about what Jesus went through with those men who followed him. One moment, His friends are celebrating Him. Later, another moment brings betrayal with His followers denying and Judas selling Him out. Jesus is crucified on the cross, and three days later, He is risen and seated on the right side of the Father. He comes back to tell the apostles they are forgiven, and He instructs them to carry the ministry that He has begun.

I searched my own heart. Here I was, proclaiming to be a Bible-reading, churchgoing, born-again Christian. Then I went through a trial, and I thought about how I could get back at those people for what they did to me. Then I received conviction in my heart for the spirit of revenge that I allowed to enter within me. I chose to forgive those who came against me, as the Lord had forgiven me.

A misconception exists that, when you receive Christ as your Savior, you enter the wonderful world of Christianity where your troubles are no more. Refiner's fire is the process of purification of precious metal by fire. It has to do with the removal of impurities that would make the precious metal less than what it should be. When believers go through a spiritual fire in life and depend on Christ for our strength, we are made stronger in our faith. Christ is transforming us through our crises and trials, and a believer must understand this. We came from a life weighed down by selfish desires, petty ambitions and amusements, and attractions in life that are temporal and not eternal. We often focus on the outer being of the person next to us instead of that person's soul. We judge by our eyes and not the value of a person as seen through God's eyes. Essentially, we don't reflect the image and glory of God in our old self.

How do we participate in this cleansing? We don't do it as much as endure it. God oversees this process in our lives. He sends us into the fiery trial, spiritually speaking, and takes us out according to His pleasure. And He does this for his glory.

What does he use to accomplish this? Without Christ, adversity, trouble, rejection, and failure can crush us, but in

Christ, we are made stronger for His glory. And people around us in these trials are watching. With the afflictions that we encounter, God is able to use them to free us from the crust, grime, and dirt of this world and our own selfishness to change us more into the likeness of Jesus.

The years since I received Christ into my heart and my life as my personal Savior have brought some tumultuous times, and many people in my life have taken notice. When I became single again, a group of men in my life gave me some of their dating advice. They declared I should live with a woman first before I marry her or not even marry her at all.

I told these men, "My desire is to please God in my life. I would not do anything that does not please Him."

That was my final answer. Well, imagine proclaiming in an honest and humble manner that I was saving myself for marriage, not self-pride. I know these men very well, and they have watched me very closely. They recognized the difference in my life before and after my faith. Some thought I changed my religion when I married this woman. They guessed I would meet another woman and change my faith again. I wasn't the only man amongst this group who had broken marriages. A few had their share of troubled relationships. I did not want to make this proclamation in a setting such as this in front of these men, but I did not want to bar the truth and deny my faith either. That was why I embraced my faith in the first place. They could not believe the words that came out of my mouth.

They exclaimed in unbelievable astonishment, "You won't sleep with a woman unless you marry her?"

I stated, "I live by the principles of the Bible, and I live to please God."

It was easier to type these words than it was to say them at the time. It wasn't easy being honest and sharing my personal life, knowing the possible backlash of teasing and mockery that may follow. But they did neither. Oh, occasionally one would razz me about this part of my life, but these guys weren't cruel. I looked at this situation as a test of my faith.

I enjoy listening to the local Christian radio station that plays contemporary positive music of faith. I was paired with a fellow worker one day. I hopped in the driver's seat and tuned the radio to my station. After a few minutes, my cantankerous but charming older partner heard what he called that "blasted church music."

He bellowed out, "I'm not listening to that #@*%$!"

So he switched the frequency to his favorite country station, which I enjoyed listening to when I was unable to tune into the Christian station. What was the station playing at the time? Part of the lyrics went, "I talk to Jesus, and I talk to God" from a popular post 9-11 song by a very familiar country and western singer.

I looked at my partner. "I thought you didn't want to hear songs about God and Jesus?"

He replied, "Well, that's different. Besides, I like country."

I just turned my head and continued to drive. Despite the differences I have with some of my colleagues at work, I don't take anything they say personally. They present mild challenges that are healthy, and God wants me to become stronger in my faith. Some Christians get too comfortable, and they want to ride the easy wave and cruise through their faith. Christianity is not without artificial believers and actors, but walking in the love of Jesus Christ and enduring our trials separates those who are real in their faith and those who are not. Jesus had His trials, and the Bible truthfully documents them.

I think many people believe that life will be peachy once they receive Christ as our personal Savior. For this reason, believers need to read and study their Bible. Becoming a believer in Jesus Christ means that you allow Him to transform your life, and when that happens, many changes will take place. People will come against you, and friends may sever ties with you once they witness the changes Christ makes in you to prepare you for your homecoming. An unbelieving family member (or perhaps spouse) will cause extreme friction with you. You no longer live a life that pleases self. You now live a lifestyle of pleasing God, a foreign concept to many people. Some may even accuse you of being in a cult, but a cult does not have a risen Savior.

Jesus carries the burdens you once did. He takes away the fear you lived in, and He fills you with His joy and abundant life. People are living a life separated from God, and now you, the believer, are living a life together with Him, so of course, those dear to you may separate themselves from you.

You will be tested, my friend, because untested faith is unreliable faith. Believers have a faith of action and firm belief that Christ will be there with you in your trial and crisis. Those who truly receive the spirit of Christ will not be crushed or defeated. Jesus will carry you through your catastrophe. He carried me through my troubles and crises. I think about the account of Shadrach, Meshach, and Abednego, who were sent into the fiery furnace because they would not bow down to King Nebuchadnezzar.

> Then Nebuchadnezzar came near to the mouth of the furnace, and spake, and said, Shadrach, Meshach and Abednego, ye servants of the most high God, come forth, and come hither. Then shadrach, Meshach, and

21

Abednego came forth of the midst of the fire. And the princes, governors, and captains and the kings counselors, being gathered together saw these men, upon whose bosies the fire had no power, nor was a hair of their head singed, neither were their coats changed, nor the smell of fire had passed on them (Dan. 3:26–27).

God did not stop the situation for these men. Instead, He changed these men in the situation because they allowed the God of heaven to work through them. We may not go through physical fire in life, but we do have those mental and spiritual fires that leave us feeling burned. God will not remove our situation; however, if we allow Him to work through us, He changes us for that situation. People have the choice to recognize the God of heaven in our lives or to deny Him.

I vividly recall one situation or trial, as I'd like to it, in the same year I received Christ as my Savior. It was June, and my department was paving a section of town roadway that intersected with a state-maintained roadway. I had been on the job for ten years at that time so I had enough experience to manage heavy traffic control operations. I should note that, while I can successfully direct traffic, the problems are the uncooperative and irate attitudes and distracted motorists we highway traffic controllers have to deal with.

Three flagmen were required for the assignment. I was one of the selected traffic safety personnel. The biggest problem was that one of us would have to stand underneath the traffic light at the four-way intersection. I was chosen to take on this position, and it has been etched in my mind like the carved words on a stone tablet. A police officer was called to stand by at the corner of the intersection in case I had trouble with any irate motorist.

I thought it would be his position to assist us in directing traffic and standing in place of the traffic light. After all, the officer had his vest, radio, club, and gun to protect him. I only had the wooden stick that my vinyl orange flag was wrapped around.

Our paving crew started at the opposite end of the road where it led into the bordering town. Everything started out organized and smooth until we reached the point where I had to take my position under the light. At that point in time, we started receiving heavy traffic from the bordering town end. The other two flagmen working with me were not seasoned traffic controllers, so they became easily panicked. The second man was walking alongside the paving machine for the safety of the men working around the equipment. The third man was posted at the end at the bordering town where we started.

Trouble did not take its time to find me. I learned a great deal about human behavior that day, and while I don't have knowledge of mental illness or disturbance, I certainly experienced some personality disturbances in some of those disgruntled drivers. I understand how discomforting it can be when you have a schedule and a highway construction entanglement is putting a kink in your daily tasks at hand. I have been in both positions so I understand the working man and woman who are only performing his or her duties. Unfortunately, it seems the rest of the general public does not share that understanding.

At my end, the traffic was backing up intensely. Not too distant from our work zone, there were two schools in two different directions. One of those schools had a bus depot where the drivers had parked the buses for the night. I knew some of the drivers. In fact, my cousin is a bus driver, so I did see some friendly faces driving school buses that day. However, I did not know some of the drivers, and they let me know how upset they were because of their long wait. But mostly only a few bus drivers gave me dirty looks, so overall, they were okay.

But the other motorists were not so merciful. I had seen most of the irate males just flip their middle fingers, which most of us can shake off. But the yelling, complaining, and cursing I often heard came surprisingly from female drivers. I have heard such profanity from some lady drivers who could make a marine drill sergeant blush.

Now I understand the stress woman are under today, running tight schedules to get their children to school before the bell and themselves to work on time. I understand the plight of the struggling single mom who has no help. But why does it seem that all of that stress is dumped on the working men and women who are performing their tasks to the best of their ability and sometimes under disorganized work conditions? I have a suggestion. Give all of your frustration and grief to God, and watch Him take care of your stressful business. Give the working man and woman a smile when you pass him or her, and let this person know he or she is doing a great job. Maybe even offer a cup of coffee. Your random acts of kindness will be returned when you least expect it.

While all this chaos and confusion was going on around me, the other two flagmen were screaming at the top of their lungs on the radio because their traffic was backing up fiercely.

"Roger, my traffic is backing up! Roger, I need to send my traffic! Rrrroooggerrrrrrrr!"

Meanwhile, I had a four-way intersection, so I was trying to send a specific number of vehicles in each direction. I was aiming for ten vehicles each way, but distracted motorists were rubbernecking to see why they were being held up. Along with all the chaos and constant yelling, my counting idea went out the window.

The officer had arrived a few minutes later after we started, and he was standing there on the corner. I decided that my orange flag was not working to my advantage, and I had more control with my hands. The average motorist knows that, when a person regulating traffic is standing in the road holding his or her hand in the "Stop" position, he or she is supposed to bring the vehicle to a complete halt. It sounds like common sense, but this idea is not foolproof.

I placed my portable radio that I was holding in my hand and clipped it to my jeans pocket. The radio was still blaring with my comrades' angry voices. I threw my flag off to the corner on the grass, but I did not pay attention to where I was aiming when I tossed it. Fortunately, I just missed the police officer.

That day, I received my fair share of belligerent drivers yelling and cursing, and I heard many comments like, "Where did you learn to @%#&&*% flag!"

The comments, angry and negative, were changed in various forms, and I might add that some people are very creative at mixing their English language with new profane vocabulary. I'm sure these angry, frustrated folks are nice, sweet human beings, but it startled me to witness human beings out of control like this.

My workday came to a close, and with me on my knees, I thanked God I survived this day. That evening, I attended a men's Bible study being held in a fellow brother's living room. I received prayer and reassurance from my brothers in Christ that they were keeping me in thought. Our discussion was about the forgiveness Jesus showed us as He hung there on the cross. Maybe this day happened for God's plan to show me humility and forgiveness. It may have been a glimpse of what Jesus went through.

Forgiveness is so difficult, but it is a vital part of the Christian life. It is also necessary if we are to be free and receive eternal life. I understand I cannot change other people's behavior. I can only control my own. No one can control me unless I give him or her the power.

No matter what trials I have faced, I never left church, even during and after the divorce. I decided to attend another church through a friend's recommendation, but this was not because of any personal animosity. On the contrary, I wanted to give my full attention and worship to God and Christ without the distraction or temptation of ill feelings. It was best for me to go to another house of worship where I could start out fresh. One direction never changed in my trials. I remained focused on God's direction for my life. I stumbled at times, and I questioned Him about what went wrong. But I never cursed God for what happened. Despite this painful event in my life, I was blessed with the ability to see through the problems in my life and to know I wasn't alone. I have my Savior to carry me through life's fiery trials.

I have also experienced transformation. When I became a father, I first took a vow I made to my unborn child that he or she would never have to suffer a life with an intoxicated and embarrassing father. Sobriety gave me a new outlook on life, and I gained precious quality time to spend with my daughter. I also curbed my profane mouth for so long a time when she was an infant that, when she started talking, it became natural for me to speak in her presence without a curse word rolling off my tongue. I did not want my daughter using that language or speaking God's name in a profane or blasphemous manner like I used to do. I have been told that she will still hear curse words on the school bus or other places. I believe that, as long as I set the right example and choose to be a better influence in her life, she will know what is both hurtful and helpful to say.

A positive and inspiring adult influence can change a child's life direction toward greatness, but a negative and downcast adult influence can be disastrous to a child's life. I never realized how many people curse God and Jesus. They don't even know they are doing it. Maybe they do and have no reverence. My employment in road construction tested my ability to stay focused and to honor and love God by speaking words of love and encouragement. Occasionally I have slipped, and my fellow co-workers have humorously chided me.

They would say comments like, "Hey, Reverend, you better go to church and repent that mouth of yours!"

I needed to spend time with other believers through Bible study. Fellowshipping with my brothers in Christ assured a healthy influence in my spiritual walk. I developed a deeper respect for women, and after having conversations with Pastor Lou, I banished the pornography I owned prior to my conversion. Many men have teased me when they discovered my stance on this important moral issue. Some men I know believe it is because of my "religion" that I cannot view pornographic material. By studying the Bible, God's Word has cleaned my heart, washed my mind of mental filth, and made my eye sensitive to images that break God's heart. God made us so beautiful, and He created woman so man would not be alone. Pornography destroys what God created for man; it destroys relationships.

I once overheard one of my father's friends commenting

when Dad told his friend he caught me looking at a girly magazine when I was in my early teens.

His friend's worldly console was, "Hey, at least you know your son likes girls."

I now know that viewing this media offends God and breaks his heart because it violates and harms the human body that is His creation. The only naked woman God willed for man to see is the man's own wife. Men are visual, and any thought that grows, rooting in our minds, can become action. To say that pornography is harmless is a deceitful and dangerous lie. Hasn't history taught us that human beings are capable of ungodly acts toward humanity? Those acts are born in our minds, just like any idea is. The women in those magazines made a wrong choice, and now male eyes and minds, from young to old, view this media. God made us so beautiful, and we are to be loved in a proper way. God made Eve for Adam so a man would not have to live alone. So God made one man for one woman, a companionship. My heart has been redeemed, my mind has been cleansed, and my eyes are open to the truth. God creates women beautiful; pornography destroys that beauty.

When is man going to wake up, listen to God, and realize the gift we have in all women? They are precious beings we need in our lives. God did not create them for mankind to degrade. But that is a man's choice, to either protect the creation God blessed us with or to destroy them through wicked self-pleasure by our own choice.

Before I chose this sanctified way of life, my life was all about me. When I received Christ as my Savior, my lifestyle changed from living for myself to living my life to please God. That is defined as doing things that glorify God, not me. I learned to let God work through a servant like me instead of me doing good deeds to make myself look good. I learned from the Bible that most of profanity I used was blaspheming God and dishonoring women. Jesus stated in Mark 7:20 "What comes out of a man makes him unclean." That's just one scripture out of numerous verses of the bible that shows what ill we have in our hearts is spoken through our mouths. Now if you hit my hand with a hammer, of course, I may expel a curse word from my mouth. I may react to pain, but I will repent.

When a person reads the Bible, the Word of God is more convictive and corrective. I can tell just by reading about God's nature that my former vices displeased Him without needing to look up the exact verse on that issue. I try with all my heart to give my daughter proper guidance and direction. She continually seeks my approval and my knowledge of life, to which I confess I still have much to learn.

Life is a continuous journey of learning. Having cognizance of this, I strive to be a godly father for her. As the man in her life, I am a role model, and realizing this helps me to toe the line as her dad. I shared the importance of having a relationship with Christ with my daughter, along with why it is so important to have belief and faith in Christ. I have explained to my daughter that her father is not perfect and I will make mistakes as everyone does, even when I give something my best try. When I do mess things up, she forgives me. There are people in my life, a few who are very close friends and even my boss, whom I have wronged in my walk of faith, and they have forgiven me. I can only hope and pray that others can forgive me for trespassing against them.

I continue to struggle with problems in my life; however, I can react in self-centeredness or respond in Christ. In areas of my life where I have conflict, I believe it is a test of my faith, along with what I truly believe in. Do I trust in my own strength, or do I trust in God to give me strength? My difficulties remain in my life; however, I manage these problems to the best of my strength and ability. What I cannot handle, I let go and give it to God. I have realized that I am not a superhero, but I do have a loving God who spiritually resolves the battles I cannot handle alone.

Christianity is a faith of servanthood. When I'm talking to a friend or someone I just met, I keep myself sensitive to him or her, especially if he or she mentions a problem or crisis he or she is going through. I'll ask that person if I can pray over him or her right there on the spot. "Whom they set before the apostles, and when they had prayed. They laid their hands on them" (Acts 6:6).

Pastor Lou taught me about evangelism. Pastor Tony, my present teacher of the Word, explained in his Sunday messages that, as Christians, we are called to evangelize and offer prayers of healing to those who share their personal life and health concerns with us. This is our call to serve. We do not force or trick people to make decisions in faith. We present the good news of salvation through Christ to them. God is given the glory for the conversion, healing, and new life in Christ that the person receives. We don't fail in our testimony if we faithfully present the gospel and the person is not converted. We only fail if we don't faithfully present the gospel at all.

I have met people who are amazed that I will offer them hands-on prayer. I never did this before because I was not taught to do it. It seemed to me that I was supposed to keep my faith to myself. However, God has great news of redemption, salvation, and freedom for His children that it cannot be kept to oneself. Faith in Christ is not self-religion. It is having a personal relationship with God.

God has blessed my life in so many ways, including the privilege of being a dad. He has also blessed me with long-term employment and a boss who appreciates my accomplishments in my tasks. God is in control. He really is. God gave me a better understanding of respecting women through my daughter. He created man to be protectors of women, but unfortunately, it is a man's choice to abuse women. God is love. If God is not in a man's heart and mind, then what influences are absorbing our minds? I keep myself in check all the time, meaning how I treat my daughter with love, respect, and dignity. It saddens me to think about daughters whose fathers have abandoned them. They have to look to an outside man as a father figure. Your daughter is a child of God. What you do to her you also do to God.

The Scripture tells us that we are all children of God. "How great is the love the Father has lavished on us, that we should be called children of God" (1 John 3:1). And that is what we are. The first time I read this verse, I realized that, when you hurt someone, you are also hurting God. Before this life change, I recall some words that used to fly out of my ungodly mouth. Those words were demeaning and hurtful to women, and my mental image of women was not healthy. I wasn't always a gentleman in my mind or in my heart. I never hit a woman. I would never dishonor my father.

He had a man-to-man talk with me one day when I was about thirteen. He sat down with me and began speaking reverently about women.

"Son, a woman may make you very angry." Then he got nose to nose and looked right into my eyes sternly. He continued in a low voice, "You don't ever hit a woman ever. Men are to protect women, both physically and virtuously."

31

I never forgot that talk with him that day. My father was gentle with my mother, my family, and me. There was no violence in him, so I never learned to be forceful.

Other male influences were in my life though, and indecent thoughts of women would fill my mind at times. My mind was always on my own pleasures, that is, who could please me. I never thought about how my actions affected other people or what negative or positive impact I might have in someone's life. I never had someone looking up to me as a role model, as my daughter does. My father wasn't perfect. He had his faults, but he was able to show me discipline without physical abuse, all with the love and caring of a father. He grew up old school, where men did not cry, but I witnessed his tenderness. I have inherited this character trait, and I have shown with my daughter. My past choices were always aimed at taking care of me first, but that has changed. God gets the credit and glory for that! Today, I am a man is who able to teach my daughter and raise her to respect herself. I have taught her to ask questions when something seems out of order.

Today, our world is definitely out of order. I encourage her to make choices that will take her in the right direction, to accept nothing less than honor, dignity, and decent character conduct from a boy or anyone else for that matter. I wonder if there are any dads out there raising their sons to be men of honor. Any man with physical ability can father a child, but a dad can raise a young man of faith and honor. Will there be a young man of decent moral character for my daughter when she reaches the age to make that choice?

Another area of my life that changed was my involvement in politics and social standards. Before I received Christ and read His Word, I did not have any particular political or worldview.

Only when I studied the Bible did I learn the importance of biblical knowledge, and my personal views changed. I became aware of vital issues in our political system that we, the free citizens in our great country, have control over. Other people's opinions had always influenced my view of politics. I never had an opinion of my own or made my own choice without someone else's approval or persuasion over my choice. I am more involved in political views, no matter how dirty and vile this system is, especially around election time.

The American taxpaying, voting citizens are responsible for electing officials who will speak our thoughts in our absence and not do our thinking for us. We are free-willed people, not puppets. I am aware of social issues that affect marriage education and family principles.

My faith has also transformed me personally in the way I treat the environment. Before, I always took for granted this great planet God made. One day, I observed a bird's nest up close. Upon inspection of all the materials God gave birds to use in building the nest, there was one man-made piece of material, a used, yellowish piece of filter from a cigarette butt. Not only this appalling discovery, but the garbage dumped along our roadways is sickening and uncalled for.

A friend of mine vacations in the Carolinas every summer, and he has witnessed chain gangs, convicts outside along the highways, cleaning garbage. He told me he was stuck in traffic and observed that these imprisoned men appeared to be happy and joyful that they were outside, making their country look beautiful. Here in the Northeast, you don't see scenes like that. Cleaning garbage is an inhumane act to place upon someone, and it is not the most desirable position in life. Well, if we humans dirty our own backyard, who is willing to clean it up?

We either don't realize or just don't care how we impact the environment around us. Our wildlife is suffering because of human carelessness and recklessness. Becoming a dad changed the way I see my environment around me. I make sure I clean whatever area I am using, and I know my daughter is watching my example. Everything I do affects the people and our surroundings.

Most domesticated pets, like cats and dogs, will bury their waste or at least try to cover it up. Yet civilized human beings continue to throw out their trash from their vehicle windows. It is no wonder we have diseases when we leave a breeding ground for them. God created the earth. Then He created all wild animals and creeping things. He created man to have dominion over all creatures. Dominion is defined as to rule with or power to rule. Lest we forget that with great power comes great responsibility.

My faith has brought maturity and responsibility, along with consideration to the spiritual needs of others. My daughter needs a thoughtful father in a thoughtless world. I recall the days when she first began to ask "why" questions. Why this? And why that?

I would ask myself, "When do these questions stop?"

One day, God brought up a memory in my mind of times I asked, "Why?"

Some adults in my life gave this dreaded reply, "Because I said so. That's why."

To a child who is learning and growing, this is not an answer. A child's growing mind needs to be nourished with the knowledge that comes from his or her parent or immediate family. Now children can ask repetitive questions, and you can only answer so many. The point is that parents encourage their children to ask questions. They should be tuned in to important questions that are mixed in with silly questions.

I talked with my daughter about what questions she should ask. I also counseled her to observe her surroundings and think of what does not make sense or what she does not understand. I explained that any question that may affect her health and well-being are also favored. If a child does not receive a proper answer from his or her parents or family members, he or she may choose someone less than friendly who can answer his or her questions. The adult answer "because I said so" does not supply information, what children are looking for. Children should get the right information instead of getting wrong and harmful information from a stranger.

I remember the questions my daughter had in her early years were elementary in nature. While she cerebrally develops in knowledge and maturity, her curiosity brings forth questions that become deeper in her observation of life. Occasionally, she will stump me with something, and I'll reply that I don't have the answer. Then we search the dictionary, go to the Internet, and then, if necessary, back that information with the Bible if it is an area of morals and principles. Thank God for the information age, providing we get the correct information. That is why I end with the Bible.

For the ten years I have walked in my new life through Christ, it has not been an easy road. I have faced challenges, trials, and testing. I have survived and thrived successfully in faith, and I give the glory to God. I once heard a pastor on a radio program say that untested faith is unreliable faith. I have found this to be sure and true. When we focus on God, we survive and thrive within the Lord who is directing us.

I have, at times, had disparagement and questions from

nonbelievers who do not understand this life of faith I have chosen. I have made plenty of mistakes and hurt quite a few people. This will happen because we still have a fallen nature even though we have been forgiven. When we live to please God, we sin less. When we stay in the Word of God, we are blessed with having remorse for our unwise actions.

I have two broken marriages, the second by which I was blessed with a beautiful child. Some people have alienated me for the decisions I have made. Despite my fallen nature, I have continued to follow Christ, and I have never missed a Sunday service to praise and glorify God, no matter what my situation in life is. Let me clarify. I have had plenty of days of doubt where I felt God abandoned me, and I have questioned why these events happened in my life. These circumstances only made me more determined in my relentless perseverance to pray harder. When I'm between a rock and a hard place, I find a quiet place and give myself time to pray. Prayer requires belief, patience, and, spiritually speaking, a heart for God. God continues to use hardships to strengthen my faith. I made this prayer when I have troubling times, and I share it with you.

> *Lord, I will pray to you fervently. If I don't receive an immediate answer, I'll keep knocking on your door in prayer. When all I hear is silence, I will give praise knowing that an answer and a blessing follows.*

I also believe in unanswered prayers, and I have accepted them. There is a good reason for it, and we just have to trust God. He has answered my prayers through other people. I have also witnessed signs that can only be from God. One of the countless ways He works is through other people. He can even use nonbelievers to bless believers.

Christ is the saving grace when you come to that point in your life where you are broken and lonely. Perhaps you are in a place of abandonment and betrayal of lies. You are at a crossroads, one of two paths to choose from, a life serving Christ or a life serving self-desires. You have only one choice to make. Open your heart spiritually to God and allow the Lord to remove your broken past so He can reside in your heart and direct your life. Or you can remain hardened to God and refuse to believe that He can change your life. Remember, he created us with the ability to make our own decisions. I would not trade this walk for anything because I have a purpose of servanthood. I used to expect others to serve me, but now my call is to serve other people and their spiritual needs. If I just focus on serving other people through my faith with action, God will take care of my needs. He always has and always will. I have received many unexpected blessings from God.

Not all blessings are about money. Friendship, parenthood, God bringing your companion into your life, and a broken bond between a parent and a child are all blessings that money cannot buy. I understand why God hasn't made my life in faith easy. If He did, I would never get out of my comfort zone. Sometimes when you are on a long-standing break, you fall asleep in your faith, and as a believer, I don't want to fall asleep on my watch. Today, I stand on rock-solid values and principles to live a life that God purposed me to live. Other people did not cause the hurt in my life. Rather, it was my own rejection and ignorance toward God and the fact I insisted on my own plan. God is awesome. He is patient and forgiving, and He waited for me to make that eternal decision of faith. In my past, I listened to other people. Due to my lack of wisdom, my life turned to muck because I did things my way. When I gave my life to the Lord, He began to rebuild what the locusts have destroyed. He mended a broken man and turned his life into gold! He wants to do the same for you.

If you have never opened the Bible, you don't know God. You can reject the Bible for any reason of your choice, but until you read the Scripture, you will never know whom the God of heaven is. God is love. He does not have to reenergize or recharge. He is an endless fountain of love. God is not a curser, as so many people believe Him to be. God is full of blessing to those who receive Christ, His Son.

Any curse we have is from our own bad decision, yet God is blamed for our bad choices. Someone gets a sexually transmitted disease and blames God. God created our body for one person, a spouse, not a community of people.

Another myth about God is that we cannot be close to Him or have a relationship with Him. While it is true what the Bible says about God being perfect and without sin, it does not imply that we cannot draw close to Him. We are sinners, but we are His children. And by His grace, our souls are saved through Christ. His grace is waiting for us as we repent of our old ways and receive our new life through Christ. We can talk to God. We can even have a conversation with God. That's why prayer is a reverent heart-to-heart talk with God. You can talk to Him anytime you want, and anyone can talk to God. He is not untouchable or unreachable. We are reconciled to God through Jesus Christ. That's why a prayer to God is closed in Jesus' name. He wants to hear from you, so don't let a lie keep you from communicating with your heavenly father. "For the eyes of the Lord are over the righteous, and His ears are open unto their prayers, but the face of the Lord is against them who do evil" (1 Peter 3:12).

If your heart is open, God will speak to you; however, His ways are not our ways. Unlike us, He has patience, and we need that when we pray. God answers our prayers His way, and He may use other people to answer our prayers. God will answer in a way that is, without a doubt, Him, even though it seems to us that He is not answering at all. We go by schedules, and the needs and materials in our lives are being made convenient, instant, and disposable.

I believe prayer is a way of slowing us down in our lives to focus on our Creator, who gives us that peace and calm no mortal man can manufacture. We are asking our loving Father in heaven, who needs no sleep or a schedule, to answer our problems in human time. He sees what we cannot see. He handles problems we cannot. God wants our full attention. If we turn off other people's conversations when they don't pertain to our needs, we will do the same thing to God. Jesus said, "And all things, whatsoever ye shall ask in prayer, believing, ye shall receive" (Matt. 21:22).

When you pray with a reverent heart and believe that God listens, let the silence be the quietness of God listening and acting on your behalf. Give God time, and don't give Him time limits. Just know that He is working on your prayer. When praying for people, it may be that the spiritual condition of the person's heart is in question. For only that person who has a spiritually hardened heart can allow God to open it and receive healing and blessing. A closed, hardened heart can keep a person from receiving answered prayer, along with abundant blessings and healing. Don't deny yourself these gifts from God. Open your heart, and let Him heal you and free your imprisoned heart. Prayer is heartfelt conversation with God. It is not erratic banter; nor is it mandatory. Remember to thank God in prayer just as often as you ask for the needs of others and yourself. Just as we ask God for blessing, we can say blessing to God.

I always considered myself to have good manners, compliments of my upbringing. Of course, I have also found areas of improvement. In the past, whenever I sat down to a meal, I would just start shoveling food in my mouth. The only time I did say grace was at the Christmas and Easter dinner table. I learned to say grace before my meals from fellowshipping with brothers and sisters in Christ. When I joined them at gatherings such as Bible study and church, I observed their faith influenced manners, and we always started a meal with saying grace, which is thanking God for our meal. I now understand through His word that is by his grace we have a meal to eat.

A thought came to my mind. This may sound humorous, but give it some attention. When our stomachs are full, our bodily function of belching begins as air that we swallowed escapes, causing a belch or burp. On a related issue, I have read some books on body language and learned from my own observation that our bodies talk a language of its own. One day, I was eating lunch, and some men were eating nearby. When they were finished with their meal, a couple leaned back, and it seemed like they were having a belching contest amongst themselves. It also sounded like their bodies were bragging about how full they were. I used to do this. That's why I mentioned it. Belching is a natural bodily function; however, we can have a humble and respectful nature when we eat.

I have talked to Christian missionaries who have spent time in missions in other foreign nations with very poor food supply and no potable water to drink. We have God's blessing to be citizens in a nation with freedom and opportunity like America, where we can have a meal to eat at our pleasure. Someone please say, "Praise God." Saying grace before your meal is simply telling God that you are grateful to have His provision. I never thought about this issue before. I always took food for granted, not knowing or caring where it came from. I have learned so much about God, along with what he has provided us. At times, my heart is sad when people turn a deaf ear and reject Him, despite all our needs that He faithfully blesses. I am truly grateful for where I am right now, and I look forward to see what great wonders He will do. Our God is an awesome God!

Chapter 2

Looking for His Light

A person can be moved by the experience of Jesus Christ personally through His believers. When a person becomes a believer, he or she takes on the personality of Jesus Christ when he or she studies Him. I have studied the Bible on the character and person of Jesus Christ. I am not claiming to be a biblical scholar or an expert; however, I know that Jesus is called "the light of the world." We, His believers, are called to be His light. Believers cannot be perfect like Christ because we are sinners, but that is not an excuse not to walk in His love. I believe there are many hypocrites and backsliders in Christianity because they are not walking in the love of Christ. I believe many Christians read the Bible as a scholar and not as a humble servant. Early in my walk of faith, I erred by reading the Bible as a scholar. I would point out the sins of other people, and in thinking pompously to myself, I knew where they were going, to the lake of fire. Many Christians have this condition I call "Pentecostal arrogance," walking in the law instead of walking in the love of Jesus Christ. I also had this condition earlier in my walk of faith. Hey, believer, that stranger you are about to meet does not know Jesus Christ, God's only Son and the Savior of the world, the only one who can transform a brokenhearted human being. But that stranger will get to know us if we are in the word of God and walking in Christ's love. If we believers don't show acts of love, that person will never come to know who Jesus Christ is. Jesus is the light of the world, and believers who are in the word of God carry that light to others who are in darkness. Well, we are supposed to be walking in His light, but how many Christians are walking in the light of Christ?

A gentleman has been a longtime friend of my family. He is always there to help a friend in need. Some years ago, I asked if he could help me move my mother into her present location. He was happy to oblige us. His personality is that of a harmless practical joker. If he likes you, he will razz and tease you. He does not do it in a mean, cruel, or bullying way. It is just his way of showing you that he likes you. He can be very annoying at times, but he has never been malicious. When my lifestyle changed through my faith, my friend took notice with his eagle eyes. One day at work, he observed me bowing my head to say grace.

He asked me, "Do you have a headache?"

I replied, "No."

"I noticed that you bowed your head."

"I am saying grace."

He never saw me do this before, and he also knew from our conversation that I attended church on Wednesday for Bible study.

He asked, "Are you one of those born-again Christians?"

When I gave a simple "yes I am" he just turned his head with a frown. From that point on he anticipated my mistakes and called me on them. I do not take offense to this I look at it as accountability.

I had just accepted Christ as my Savior, but I was not prepared to handle the scoffing that comes with walking this faith. Many people scoff at Christians because they don't understand our faith. I also attribute the fact that some hypocrites calling themselves Christians have blindsided many nonbelievers. Many of these masqueraders walk in self-righteous and religious legalism. They seem to have no idea who Jesus is or how He works through love. Maybe you know someone like that, a person who lives a life of religious law but does not know how to show love or acts of agape (sacrificial) love that is the love of God. Before I chose this direction, my family friend never bothered me aside from workplace teasing, which is mild compared to being teased for my faith.

Let me make one thing abundantly clear. I do not get offended when I'm teased or mocked for my faith. There is a reason this happens, as I will soon explain.

Perhaps my friend has a dislike for born-again Christians due to a bad experience with someone posing as a Christian. Being a Christian isn't something you say. It is something you do. Religion is law without love, faith is love, and love can save us. Religious law cannot save anyone; nor can it personally transform anyone. When my friend teases me for my faith, I don't take it personally, and he is not the only one. I believe, when I'm teased or mocked, I'm being tested to see if I'm for real. If that's the case and it appears to be that way, then my faith is very real to me, and I will pass the test with God's help.

My friend did confide in me that he had a problem with born-again liars, as he calls them. He said, "They tell you what you should be doing according to the Bible, but they don't appear to practice what they preach." My theory is that he may have experienced Pentecostal arrogance, prideful believers who preach "Do what I say" they don't model Jesus Christ who led by His acts of love.

I agree there seem to be many preachers but very few teachers. Jesus was and is a teacher, and a teacher shows you how to catch fish so you can learn to catch fish and feed you and your family. It is sad that most Christians don't read their Bibles as servants and miss the point of their faith. We are to be a living testimony of the life-changing power of Jesus Christ. How can any Christian be a believer when you don't read the Word of God, what our belief is built on. Read, believe, and receive. Jesus did not complicate life. He gave us life. We are called to be the light and salt in a person's otherwise dark and bitter world. Some believers are bland and dim, so they need to be recharged and sweetened through the Word of God. We should read the Bible as servants, not judges of the law. Our faith is about a life transformed by grace and servanthood through acts of sacrificial love. The love of God is not beating someone over the head with our Bible. Reading the Bible does not make us scholars of biblical justice. Rather, the Bible is God's book of love. We need to share that love and leave the justice to God.

It is our call of duty to reach those who are not right with God, but we are to proclaim His love and redemption through Christ. There are lost and hurting people who don't know who Jesus is or what He has done. We believers understand how God through Christ can transform broken and damaged lives. With that transformation brings a joy and hope that should be shared. I did say we are to share faith, not force it. How do we know when to share it? Well, because it is God's good news, He will bless us with opportunities to share when we seek Him in prayer. People see us going out of our way, putting ourselves off to serve others in need. They want to know why we are doing this when it seems to them that we get nothing out it. Serving self does not produce a joyful life. Serving other people produces a joyful life because that's the way we were created. I used to hear a phrase often when I was younger, and I still hear it. "God helps those who help themselves."

This is not scripture. It is not in the Bible. That is a man-made phrase because mankind wants to create our own life and take all the glory for it. When we perform a random act of kindness, we are blessing someone, even when we do it secretly and we think no one is noticing. God sees everything, and when we perform an act of work out of pure agape love for someone, God sees our acts of work, love, and faith when no one else does. God works through believers to show His love for all His children. The love of Christ in us wins people over. We need to love people through our selfless acts of kindness and to pray for them without ceasing. We don't need to be perfect. Perfection does not exist. We just need to be available for the work Christ has called us to. There are lost, lonely, hurting people who need to be reached where they are. When they see us, they see something different in us. I believe they see the shadow of Jesus Christ in us.

Look in your Bible, and study Jesus. He worked while He walked on Earth—washing feet, feeding people, sharing God's good news, healing the sick, and bringing love to those who are treated unloving. We believers are His shadows, and we should be busy continuing what He began until our homecoming.

The Bible describes the apostles as ordinary fallen men who Christ called to follow Him. When push came to shove, they turned on Him after they vowed their commitment to Him. But Christ forgave them, for he knew they would fall because in our flesh we are weak. Jesus said in Matthew 26:41, " Watch and pray so that you will not fall into temptation. The spirit is willing, but the flesh is weak." Those who believe in Jesus Christ are not perfect. (I may repeat this often in the book. Practice makes improvement. Perfection does not exist in human beings.) Jesus cannot work though people who believe they are perfect or full of self and pride. Christ can only work through people who are broken and who have a sense of humility.

Jesus often had conflict with the Pharisees because they were self-righteous and without humility. They read the law and became the law instead of becoming the love of Christ. Think about the humility Jesus needed to hang on that cross and take our punishment. Today, Christ needs the same broken people who have humility to go out and reach those who are spiritually oppressed and broken in life. We often build these invisible walls of protection around our hearts. These "walls" have been built to protect us from our painful and agonizing past. These walls prevent Jesus from entering our soul to heal us. He wants us to be joyful people walking, not dead, miserable people rambling. Once these walls of pride and self are broken down, only then is Christ able to work in us, and to Him is the glory.

An effective believer must be devoted to daily prayer and Scripture reading. We must be in prayer for the needs of others. We are to show the character of Christ—His sacrificial love, compassion, forgiveness, and humility to those who don't otherwise know Jesus Christ.

Recalling my friend's animosity toward born-again Christians, I am not offended at his sarcastic negative remarks. I don't take it personally. I've known him long enough to know that he does not act this way to ridicule me. Matter of fact, I agree with my friend, and I am sure many people regard

Christians the same way. It is simply not enough to attend church and call yourself a Christian.

Our faith is all about a life of transformation. To use a metaphor, a Christian is a caterpillar whom Christ transforms into a butterfly. When a person receives Christ, he or she enters a redeemed life and a personal transformation. Our faith is about walking in love that is putting others first and ourselves second. Jesus changes a person from the inside. He cleans all the "junk" that's preventing you from having the life God intended you to have. That decision to receive a new life in Christ is up to you. I believe there are spiritually weak-hearted Christians because they have not allowed Christ to change their hearts to full-strength faith. Jesus said, "So because you are lukewarm, neither hot or cold, I am about to spit you out of my mouth" (Rev. 3:16). You either accept Christ and serve Him or deny Him and serve yourself. There is no in between. Reading the Bible is the only way to strengthen your belief and take your stand for Christ. If one is truly a believer living for Christ and Scripture is in one's heart, his or her actions of God's agape love will speak for him or her. When a person receives our act of love, he or she is usually open to hear what we have to say. Our act of love opens the door to talk personal salvation through Christ.

What exactly are acts of love? How about offering to help someone in an area he or she is struggling with? With women, it could be doing laundry and housecleaning tasks and asking about grocery needs. Help with children, especially in the situation of a husband whose career is military, firefighting, or law enforcement. Men can help other men. Treat your brother to a cup of coffee and man-to-man conversation. Ask if your brother needs help with repairs on the car or house. Speaking from a man's point of view, it is extremely difficult to ask for help. This often indicates weakness in a world that believes real men don't cry. That's why men of God need to stand together strong in the word of God. We are in a spiritual battle. Divorce divides and destroys families. Born-again Christians need to get out of their comfort zone and get involved without expecting a reward. We already have our reward now. We need to be shadows of Jesus Christ in the lives of broken people, husbands and wives, and children.

I am concerned about the servanthood of believers in America. I use the word "servant" numerous times in this book. We read and study the Bible to learn about God—who He is and what He has done for us. We attend church to give praise and glory to God. Most people do know that Jesus was a carpenter and a teacher. The Bible has much more to describe Jesus Christ other than that lackluster description. He was and is a man of action. He performed labor healing as well as fed people. The Word of God can give you a much bigger idea of Jesus Christ than I can. When he walked this earth, He worked, taught, healed, fed, laughed, cried, forgave, and died. The best news is that God raised Him from the dead, and God will do the same for us. All we have to do is ask, and we will receive. Our faith needs more believers who are willing to get their hands dirty serving people. Our Savior's hands were not idle. They became soiled while laboring for the lost. Why are we His followers any different? The Bible is our life handbook and illustrates how we are to live our faith and God's principles. The church is merely a building, a spiritual gathering place. The body of Christ is believers, not a building. Mark 16:15 affirms our call to duty. "And He said unto them 'Go ye into all the world, and preach the Gospel to every creature.'" All believers are students who need to be fervently studying the Word of God and serving Christ. No student or servant is above his or her master. To know we are those who serve a redeeming savior is to be touched by our faith in action, not by mere self-boasting words from our lips. Many claim the Christian name, but they give no selfless acts of love and sacrifice, to take time out of one's busy schedule and offer prayer and laying of hands to a hurting friend or stranger. Who is willing to visit a nursing home or a sick homebound friend who does not have a personal relationship with Christ? Are believers praying for our nation? Let us not speak judgment over our people for we also deserve that stone we hold in our hand.

In recent years, I have observed on two occasions a small group of believers praying over each other in public places. One was in the food court of the mall as I witnessed a man and woman in a circle with three other people, and this gentleman was leading with hands-on prayer. The other time, I was walking across the parking lot of a lumber supply center, and I witnessed three women praying in a circle. When I reached my car, I prayed for those three women that God would answer their prayers. That is our faith in action, taking the time from our busyness to pray over a fellow human being's needs. What seemed unusual to me as I watched these two events is that they both occurred in my home state of New York. This tender showing of our faith and concern for others is more common to see in the Bible Belt of America.

I turn to another subject that comes into question. Is our faith about financial success? Jesus said to the rich man in Mark 10:21,

> One thing thou lackest; go thy way, sell whatsoever thou hast, and give to the poor, and thou shalt have treasure

in heaven: and come, take up your cross and follow me. And he was sad at that saying, and went away grieved: for he had great possessions.

I believe the Lord is saying it is okay to have possessions as long as they don't own you. There is nothing wrong with wanting to acquire money or possessions as long as they don't become your god. In another verse, Jesus tells us that money is not the root of all evil. The love of money causes evil. "For the love of money is a root of all kinds of evil: which while some coveted after, they have erred from the faith, and pierced themselves through with many sorrows" (1 Tim. 6:10).

Money can draw believers away from the word of God, and that is when grief afflicts them. God is not against financial prosperity, but He did warn us about the love of money. Money is God's instrument to test our faithfulness and to see if we bless others or hoard our blessing. Do we use money for God's glory or our own gain? We should use a business opportunity as a blessing and chance to use our good fortune to bless others.

One good example of a blessing from a godly businessperson is the blessing of employment to a husband to provide for his family. Capitalism is opportunity to build a business in America. I believe God anointed our forefathers with the insight of a nation that can prosper from the ideas of its own citizens rather than depending on other nations for our supply. That's what capitalism does for America. For our own citizens, we provide the goods they need instead of depending on foreign supply for goods. American independence means we can depend on our own citizens. Who feeds us? Who clothes us? And who employs us? If we are an independent nation, shouldn't we be able to rely on our free citizens? Ultimately, God provides our blessings to our nation with the ability to achieve financial success. God loves America, but does America love God?

The problem with America's financial crisis is not capitalism. The problem stems from personal greed. When we love money, problems overwhelm us. When we love God by loving others in need with blessing, we are no longer prisoners of the pain that comes with greed. While writing this, I came up with a slogan, "Support capitalism in America; cancel the greed by blessing other people."

As believers, God allows us to prosper; however, we are not to forget why Christ called us to serve Him. God uses many entrepreneurial businesses for His glory. That is the key when we set out to build our own business. We do it to glorify God and be a blessing to others. Our faith is not a success seminar; churches are not country clubs. Although we can pursue financial freedom, we also have a call to be servants of the Lord and to act in His love.

Our faith and America needs believers who pray relentlessly, along with immerse themselves in the Word of God. We need believers who live a life of love, not religious law. We need to reach out to other people who are lost and lonely, the downtrodden of society. We need to get out of our comfort zone and offer prayer and a warm hug to those we meet and make them feel as though Jesus Christ Himself is embracing them because He is working through us. That is what our call is about, interceding for Christ by serving lost souls and showing our light. Our nation needs Christians who take heed to their calling. A believer is a human being, a sinner who has heard the good news of salvation through Jesus Christ. Someone shared the message of God's love and His forgiveness through His only begotten Son.

We have all traveled that path full of strife, misery, and brokenness. We can stay on that path that has left us empty, broken, and abandoned or choose God's less-traveled, uneasy road, one that builds character and courage. A person will have to adjust his or her stride for this walk and prepare himself or herself for rough terrain.

However, when we trust in the Lord, He walks side by side with us through our challenges. We will become spiritually stronger. We will also be strengthened in agape love and character to reach a strong arm to our fellow believers and nonbelievers alike. Many people have become believers through a servant who serves though action and then shares the gospel. When someone makes a personal choice to accept Christ and live this sanctified life, it is difficult to adjust from our former self-centered way of living.

Our transformation through Christ does not happen overnight. It is a gradual work; therefore, we are all works in progress. Our life is Christ-centered, that is, we do what pleases God, not ourselves. You begin to see the life, the purpose that God always wanted you to have.

You will also have civil conflict within yourself because you are now denying your self-pleasures, and our flesh does not like to be denied. Life through Christ is not a selfish lifestyle, and it goes against the "me" lifestyle that all believers came from. We have to remember that we are called to serve. When someone becomes a believer, emotionalism can override the causing of an overzealous nature and may result in a falling away of people converted superficially. When a person receives his or her conversion to Christ, he or she needs to combine his or her mind with a commitment bringing spiritual growth and a life of Christian discipleship.

Jesus was righteous because He did not sin. Our Savior spoke truth and inspiring words, and He reached out to all people, no matter their lot in life. I have observed some Christians who have carried a self-righteous attitude about themselves as though they are saved and everyone else is not. It is unfortunate that these believers are not only missing the message about winning spiritually lost people to Christ. They are also falling to their own pride.

Are we not Bible-reading believers? We should share God's message of salvation through His Son Jesus Christ with a humble nature to a lost and hurting world. There should be an excitement to read the Bible and understand the God of heaven who has been misunderstood due to man's rebellious and ignorant nature. Bible study is necessary, for God's truth is in His Word. The Bible speaks of God's wrath upon those who act in evil and work against God, a personal choice. The Bible also speaks of God's love, mercy, and forgiveness, and that is where we believers appear. We are to show God's love, mercy, and forgiveness.

Attending Bible study and participating in daily prayer are very important. Our faith is a lifestyle, just like physical fitness. To just stay in good physical condition, you must have a disciplined schedule. A new believer must be taught, encouraged, and inspired about his or her new faith. People in your life will start to see these gradual changes and question if your church is controlling you. They do not understand that biblical principles are changing you to live an abundant, Christ-filled, God-pleasing life. A caterpillar changes into a butterfly, another beautiful design by God. A person born of self-desires becomes a new creation in Christ.

So often I have heard people say that Christians are

controlled, there are certain rules and regulations we have, and the church sets them. The church is just a place where we gather to praise and worship God. A church can be a body of believers gathered in a grassy field singing praises to the Lord and learning more about God in His Word. That is church, my friend. We study together, and the lessons we learn come straight from the Bible, the Word of God.

As for what we can and cannot do in our lives, God is specific. We may live a life that pleases him and one that our bodies were originally made for. God created our bodies for His and our healthy pleasure. We create problems when we use our bodies for our unhealthy pleasure. Without God in our lives, we are insatiable beings, and nothing will satisfy or complete us. His principles change our lives and give us the life he intended. Only Jesus Christ can give us eternal salvation (eternal life). A believer can do anything that glorifies God. Whatever we want to do—read a book, see a movie, listen to music, speak a language, or socialize somewhere—we can do it as long as we glorify God. We don't have to please God, and we are not forced to live this way. Glorifying God and having a relationship with our Creator who loves us is a choice. We were made to love and adore Him. We don't have to. We who receive Him want to. We have the grace of God and the hope of eternal life through Christ who is in our lives.

Jesus Christ began His ministry and commanded His disciples to carry it on. The New Testament of the Bible records His ministry. We show our faith when we perform acts of kindness and sacrifice our time for the benefit of others. This is called agape love, God's love. We believers have our reward in heaven through Jesus Christ so we don't have to do good works. We do good works for other people because we are acting in service for God. We should be doing it with a joyful, not burdensome, attitude.

Have you ever had someone pray over you at the mention of your problems or crisis? Christ called us to do this, as His disciples and we believers show God's love when we do this. Do people see that special difference in us that is Christ, or do they see a person whose life is characterized by that phrase, "Do as I say not as I do"? If our lifestyle is dedicated to Christ, we will win the lost, but if our lives are lived in contradiction of our faith, people will see right through us. They won't see Christ. Let our actions of love speak our faith.

Bumper stickers are a popular way of expressing ourselves in humorous political statements and words of wisdom. I have noticed an abundance of bumper stickers on vehicles from commercial to personal cars. One sticker tends to stand out from the rest. It has a symbol of the cross or fish on it, the Christian bumper sticker. These symbols tell us that the person who owns and operates this vehicle is a Christian. Upon taking notice of this symbol, you would think that this vehicle's driver is displaying Christlike behavior. Now we are not perfect people; however, we are supposed to be thoughtful of others, and we are the first impression of Christ to those who don't know Him.

When I see this symbol on a vehicle and the driver is on his or her cell phone or cuts me off in traffic, it disturbs me. Yes, we are imperfect, but to display a symbol that indicates the driver is a believer in Jesus Christ, our Lord and Savior, and then shows carelessness for others on the road, we wonder why people have attitudes toward Christians. If you are not ashamed to proclaim His name on your vehicle, then go ahead and display it just as long as what you believe is consistent in how you live. We are better off showing people who we are by helping others with work and prayer than by showing material signs of our faith and forgetting we are publicly showing them. So go ahead and place your sticker, and then wear your shirt. Just don't forget who you are representing. How can we win people over to our Savior when His believers are acting in a thoughtless manner like the rest of the world? We are supposed to be different because Christ is in us.

Personally speaking, it is not easy being a Christian on the road today. Trust me. I am tested at every street corner. The area I live in, although it is a suburban part of the state, is very congested on a traffic level. There are rough roads and constant road repairs due to the heavy traffic volume. When you add distracted drivers to these situations, it becomes very difficult to maintain a patient, calm, godly attitude during stressful highway traffic congestion. Thank God I can listen to the local Christian radio station in my area, broadcasting positive music and messages in a discouraging and distracted world.

If you cannot get a radio station like this, I would suggest preparing for your trip by supplying yourself with inspirational music. Or maybe purchase a compact disc with your favorite teacher of the Word of God. If we focus our minds on Christ, there is less tendency to lose our patience, which gives fuel to rage. I have been told I drive like a slowpoke, although I do maintain the posted speed limit. I have also completed the defensive driving course that teaches a motor vehicle operator to be responsible for his or her own driving actions. The drivers who hold a commercial driver's license at my workplace are required to take this class. In my opinion, all motorists should be required to do the same.

I haven't exceeded the posted speed limit since my active days in the volunteer fire department. I have a true story I want to share with you. Five years prior to my decision to live for Christ, I was out for the evening with some friends. On the way home, one of my friends and I were waiting at a traffic light on a four-lane highway not far from our town. We were making a left turn onto a road that merged from four lanes into two-way traffic. My friend and I both owned fairly new pickup trucks. Both were eight cylinders. He had a diesel engine; I had a gas engine. Prior to this night, we had previously questioned each other which one of our trucks would win a drag race.

The moment came when we were side by side at the traffic light in double left-hand turning lanes. We both looked around carefully and did not see a patrol car in sight. We stared at each other as we revved our engines, nudged our vehicles forward, and exchanged challenging smirks, instigating a drag race. The left-turning red arrow changed to a green arrow, and I accepted the dare by slamming my foot on the gas pedal to the floor. My friend responded likewise, and the piercing sound of screeching tires broke the quiet midnight air. I could see the smoke from our burning tires in my rearview mirror. I can still hear the startling sound of our racing, screeching tires. Before we hit the quarter-mile mark, I was ahead when my heart almost jumped out of my chest as flashing lights danced in my rearview mirror and my speedometer read eighty miles an hour in the posted zone of forty miles an hour. The officer pulled alongside my friend, and the officer told my friend to follow him as he went after me. I had already pulled myself off to the side.

My father once gave me some good life advice. If an officer is pursuing you, whether you are right or wrong, don't run. In this situation, I was completely wrong. I watched as the officer spoke to my friend. I stared in the mirror, shaking feverishly and feeling scared out of my skin while waiting for him to approach.

He cautiously walked up to my truck. "License and registration." He paused while I searched for my documents. "Why were you going so darn fast?"

I honestly replied, "Officer, I'm wrong. I wanted to see what this truck could do."

"What is the blue light on your dashboard for?'"

"I'm a volunteer firefighter."

He replied, "You should know better!"

He held my license like he was not going to give it back. "Where do you live?"

I gave him the address.

He slowly reached out his hand toward me and handed my license back to me. "Good. Go home and stay there for the rest of the night."

I did exactly as the officer recommended, and my friend followed behind me. The next day my friend told me the officer asked him why we decided to race pick up trucks in front of him. My friend told him we didn't see a patrol car in sight. The officer revealed, "I was parked on the hill in the bank parking lot and you looked over but obviously not far enough". To his chagrin my friend answered, "If we knew you were there we wouldn't have raced." The officer gave him his license back and sternly suggested he go home. I was very foolish that night. I only thought about myself. I put four people in danger that night in my selfish follies: the officer, my friend, my first ex-wife, and myself. Yes, she was in the truck with me that night. She had a few quiet but stern words to say to me. After that, silence filled the cab of our truck for the remainder of our trip home. She didn't have to say anything more for fear and guilt riddled my face and my body. That was my first and last time drag racing, and I hoped I never had to see that officer again.

The following weekend, my fire chief asked if I'd like to drive our fire engine in the parade. I was excited to be given that opportunity. On the day of the parade, when our company came to end of the marching line into the fairgrounds, I parked the engine on the carnival grounds where other departments parked their apparatuses. I locked the cab doors of the fire engine.

I told my chief, "I parked the shiny, red and white pumper and locked it."

To my chagrin, he put his head down with a half-grin and half-frown. "The lock is broke. You weren't supposed to lock the cab door."

My chief proceeded to find a police officer on the carnival grounds with a device to unlock the door of our fire engine. Moments later, he came back with an officer. Guess who the officer was? I kept my distance, and he didn't say anything. He just helped us out and went on his way. Let my embarrassment be a lesson to anyone. My foolish ways could have harmed many people that night.

By the grace of God, my dangerously foolish days are behind me. My faith has changed my thoughtlessness to a deep concern for careful driving over that of my youthful rashness and immaturity. There are so many people on the road with school buses picking up children, delivery trucks, and garbage removal. Lest we forget the animals crossing busy highways. Other than a legal racetrack, where in America can you race at your vehicle at the top speed without the risk of causing casualty to other people or colossal property damage? Here's something to ponder the next time you are being delayed. Maybe that delay, whether it be on the road, in the grocery store line, or elsewhere in your schedule, is a divine appointment trying to divert your premature arrival to heaven.

My pastors and fellow believers have encouraged and inspired me to stay in the Word of God, my Bible. Church service is on Sunday and Wednesday evenings. Why do we go twice a week? Isn't once enough? Attending church is not an obligation. It is spiritual energizing, especially if you had a rough week of life. It is a time to hear worship music, to get in the Word of God, and to give Him praise. Going to Wednesday evening Bible study recharges and restores a believer and gives us fellowship with other believers. Weekly lessons to learn about God's nature and to grow close to Him are not enough.

Bible study is a lifestyle, and fellowshipping with other believers encourages us in our walk of faith. I carry my Bible everywhere I go. It is an important part of a believer's life. We are modern-day apostles. What we live today, they also lived. The times, technology, and clothes have changed, but selfishness, hurt, and fallen human nature have not changed at all. The Bible is like no other book written. When a person opens the Bible, begins to read it with an open mind and a heart, and desires to know God, the Word reads like a live-action story.

I have been asked if I find the Bible complicated. Yes, at times, I do find some of the words dense, and it does sound strange because of the ancient language. However, when I pray for understanding before reading, my mind is open, and I read through it. Often times, the difficulty I experience is a lesson speaking to me that I might not want to hear. At times, the Bible speaks conviction to my fallen nature for doing something that displeases God, such as not seeking forgiveness during a personal conflict with someone. I will also ask the Lord in prayer for the meaning to what I have read, and the application for my life is revealed to me. I find comfort in reading about the life of Jesus and the men who followed Him.

The women in the Bible are also important. Jesus did not limit His ministry to men. Mary Magdalene and the other Mary, the first to arrive at the empty tomb, were involved in ministry. The Bible has the answers, but sometimes we may be ready to hear it. Or perhaps God has to do some work in us in order for the answer to work in our lives.

Humility is a part of our walk of faith, and it is a difficult characteristic to show when we are still dealing with our boastful pride. Jesus was not and is not arrogant. In all His heavenly majesty on this earth, he reached out to every lost and hurting soul, from the diseased leper to the Samaritan woman at the well who received His compassion and forgiveness. Today, many lost people need a loving hand to hold or someone to hug them and to tell them that they are loved and will be okay.

But where are these servants for whom lost souls can find the salt, light, and love of Christ? Are they turning arrogant, causing them to turn their noses on the downtrodden? If we are not in our Bibles and humbling ourselves before the Lord, we will backslide to our self-centered nature. We can remain strong in our walk of faith by joining others in ministries.

Speaking of believers, how are churches faring toward worship and teaching the salvation through Jesus Christ? We loved to be entertained, and with God's blessing, we can use any reasonable resource as long as we glorify God and show others how we live a life of love.

Some churches have used entertainment to present the gospel message. I read a recent news article about a mega church of colossal structural proportion and a congregation with a population to fill it. They spent a great deal of money on Christmas and Easter plays with live animals in the scenes. Using extravagant resources like this is wonderful to present the message of Christ. That church is now in financial uncertainty, although there may be more to the problem than costly productions. There is nothing wrong with grand productions to champion the message of salvation.

There are also simple ways of opening doors to people to share the message of salvation. Offering a hot cup of coffee on a cold day to someone we see every day but don't know his or her name or a friend works wonders. Ask a friend or co-worker how his or her life is, and perhaps treat him or her to a modest lunch.

I know one church that put on some inspiring Easter productions, and they stayed within their financial budget by using congregants who were all willing to volunteer as actors. They literally took a crash course in acting. The novice assembly of thespians gave a great performance, and many of these annual shows touched people who came to see it. Members of the congregation even volunteered their talents in building the various scenes. Everyone in the production prayed before the show that the message of salvation through Jesus Christ would forever touch at least one person. There is nothing wrong in entertaining visitors coming to see a church theatrical production as long as we remember that we are in the soul business, not show business.

I am very fond of the motorcycle ministry. I have been a fellow biker for many years. You probably would not associate bikers with church or having anything to do with God. But that is the purpose of such ministries. When a group of bikers, for whatever reason, cannot or will not come to church, the church goes to them. That's what Jesus did. He reached out to the multitudes. But the choice to receive Him when he knocks on the door of your heart is yours. Can you picture a man or woman dressed in leather going to church on a bike, especially when the norm is to go in your Sunday best?

Leather is the Sunday best for a biker. Imagine what it might have been like if motorcycles were around in biblical times? What a glorious site to behold Jesus riding into Jerusalem on His hog. Back when I had a more flexible schedule, I had the opportunity to go on rides with the Christian Motorcyclist Association (CMA). The chapter I rode with is called Ezekiel's Wheels. The name is from the book of Ezekiel in the Bible.

I have met some fascinating people from all walks of life and various workplaces. Motorcycles bring people together. No matter where you come from, every man and woman loves the rumble of a motorcycle engine and the wind in his or her face. On occasion, we had the honor of a deputy sheriff escorting us through some local rides in neighboring towns. Men and women of this ministry gather at community events, sharing the freedom of riding and the love of Christ with others. I have never witnessed a group of bikers out in a park or a field, just taking in the soulful, refreshing breeze of spring, summer, and fall while they sit together in silent prayer. The presence of God surrounds you throughout the time you behold leather-clad men with the Lord's compassion in their hearts praying over each other. These ministries are able to reach out to a community of people no one else may dare to. Believing bikers have opportunities to go to those who would never go to a church. They are able to connect with fellow bikers without misunderstanding because they know and appreciate what being a biker is all about.

Men and women of all occupations can relate to the biker life, even if riding is a part-time hobby from busy schedules. The biker life represents freedom to roam our great countryside and explore the beauty of our great nation. There is no pressure, time clocks, and schedule. We get to our destination when we get there. We don't always have a plan, but we'll figure it out as we go, and we'll make new friends along the way. Various ministries can reach people in so many areas of society if there are willing servants. The harvest is plenty, but the workers are few.

I have many brothers in the Lord who encourage me to study the Bible, and we talk about the men of the Bible, especially the apostles who were no different than today's men. A friend once talked about the way Jesus has been portrayed in paintings. Most of these portraits seem to imply that Christ was of a meek and soft nature. You never see Jesus the carpenter or traveler in these paintings; you never see the ruggedness of His character. After all, He did take on human flesh. The Bible tells of a man contrary to that canvas depiction.

He was and is the perfect man, and the Scripture tells us that He was is and always will be relatable to man's problems. He was a biblical scholar, the great physician, a working man, and a Savior to those who received Him. He was not idle. His hands were always working and healing, and they still are. Jesus was a servant among His chosen twelve disciples and many others. He spoke the word of God with authority, and He washed the feet of His brothers.

Christ even experienced anger. The Word tells us one moment in the life of Christ where He overturned the tables at the temple where merchants gathered to gain profit. They sold sacrifices at exorbitant prices and cheated worshippers who came to give God praise and glory. Jesus became upset because of what the money changers were doing.

And Jesus went into the temple of God, and cast out all them that sold and bought in the temple, and overthrew the tables of the moneychangers, and the seats of them that sold doves, and said unto them "It is written, My house shall be called the house of prayer, but ye have made it a den of thieves" (Matt. 21:12–13).

He was angry because the temple was a holy dwelling place for His Father, and these shopkeepers were turning it into a defiled marketplace. According to the Bible, Jesus never physically struck anyone. The only violence in Jesus' life was that which all of mankind placed on Him at the cross. He instructed believers on what to do when someone comes against us. "But I tell you, do not resist an evil person. If anyone slaps you on the right cheek, turn to them the other cheek also" (Matt. 5:39).

We are not to turn to violence but flee from it and pray fervently that God will deliver us from that situation. The latter verse talks about not taking revenge when someone comes against us. We are allowed to protect ourselves when we are cornered in a hostile situation and have no way out. We are not to seek revenge, but we are not supposed to be doormats either. We have the right to defend ourselves against physical harm.

I was curious about the word "love" because of the fact it is such an overused English word. My research on the word "love" came up with very insightful results. In the English language, the word "love" is defined as a strong liking for someone and an affection for one person toward another. My inquiry further led me to the Greek language, where love is defined in various forms. In our society, the word "love" describes one emotion for every affection, but not all our elations of fondness and joy are expressed the same way. We love our mates, children, jobs, cars, and homes, but not all in the same expression.

The Greek word "agape" is the most common form of love in the Bible, and the Bible defines it as a selfless, sacrificial, unconditional love, the highest of the four types of love in the Bible. It is comparable to the sacrificial love a parent has for his or her child, regardless of whether such love is reciprocated. This love drives one to save the helpless, even driving one to help one's enemies. Agape love focuses on how you can meet the other person's needs. In our society, if two men meet and say they love each other in public, it is often assumed in a sensual manner. Two believing men can say "I love you, brother" without any misunderstanding of gender attraction. In some cultures, a man kissing another man on the cheek is a form of phileo (brotherly) love and is honored as friendship. In American society, however, a man kissing another man on the cheek is interpreted as eros (sensual, of the flesh) love and not phileo love.

The night before my father died suddenly of his aneurysm, he expressed his paternal joy in the way I made wise choices. He told me that, at times, he was concerned with the youthful crowd I associated with, thinking they might have influenced me. I admit I hung around the teens who drank and smoke because they accepted me. They didn't treat me like a misfit loser, like the preppy and scholarly teens did. I only drank alcohol. I didn't get involved in smoking any of that mind-controlling stuff, although alcohol is a mind controller. My father brought me up to respect and serve my country. He often brought me to the volunteer fire station where he performed much voluntary services, such as being a handyman. When I turned sixteen, he encouraged me to join as a junior member. So at the age of sixteen, I was associated with other men of the department, and we worked closely with the police department. My fellow firefighters and the police officers liked me so I didn't want to do anything that would mess up my association with them. I did not want to let my father down. I could be very honest with him. He was strict and firm but never bullheaded or hardnosed like some other fathers I have known.

My dad kissed me on the cheek three times in my life, including that night when I dropped him off at home after receiving an award from the same volunteer station we were members of. Before I left, he hugged me and kissed me on the cheek for the last time.

The department gave him a beautiful tribute with a fire truck carrying his casket to the cemetery and another fire engine carrying the floral arrangements. My mother was honored as the wife of a firefighter and past chief. The funeral director asked if I wanted the funeral procession to travel past the fire station where he was the chief in 1966, the year I was born. I agreed to the idea, and when the combination of fire department and vehicles drove past the volunteer firehouse in tribute, one of the members set off the loud mechanical siren (like an air raid siren) that sat on top of the utility pole. The firehouse whistle, a device that calls all firefighters to alert, sang her song to dad for the last time.

I was a second lieutenant fire officer. I did not have a relationship with God at that time in my life, but He was watching over my family and me and waiting for me to call Him into my life. I was sad for a while over suddenly losing my father, but I recovered from the grief and continued to carry on. I am so grateful to God that He gave me a chance to say good-bye to my dad. So many sons live with regret of never having the chance to tell their dad they love them.

Maybe you and your dad don't have the same bond I had with my father. You have unforgiveness and bitterness that you cannot bury the grudge. Your heavenly Father wants to have that bond you didn't receive. It is not easy being a father, trying to be a role model in a society that does not help a father to be a dad and a good example. I know some friends who say it is not easy being a son, trying to make your dad proud of you, especially if you have a dad who cannot be won over no matter what you do. A few friends of mine spent their lives trying to win their father's favor and sacrificed matters in their life to win their father's love but to no avail.

Our society does not promote principles for men to be honorable fathers. Neither are sons and daughters taught or influenced to respect their parents. If there is ever a good reason to need God in your life, it is when you need a father figure. I write this from one son to another who is reading this, but I am also speaking to daughters who may have a relationship problem with their mothers. I give the same advice to daughters as I do to sons. Our society is neither kind nor spiritually helpful to parents.

Communication and respect for our elders is mutual. Sons and daughters, you don't get respect. You earn it. If you don't have parents, come to God's family, and He will provide. An organization called Focus on the Family has great resources to help you in your time of need. Look them up on the Internet.

Maybe you're thinking there's no hope of reconciliation between your father and you. Don't let regret and guilt control your life. Make amends even if it is not mutual. If your parent is relentless in his or her grudge, let go and let God work on his or her cold, resentful heart problem. But know and understand this. Your heavenly Father forgives and loves both of you!

When I think about this agape love that Jesus showed toward us, our soldiers, firefighters, and police officers come to my mind. In any situation of turmoil, a soldier never leaves another behind. That principle and creed also bonds with firefighters and police officers. War, fire, and civil disturbances are hostile and turbulent situations. Men and women who answer the call to serve are unique individuals. Not all people are cut out to do these lines of work. It takes a special selfless person to sacrifice all he or she accomplished to help his or her fellow comrade, even if the situation ends with one's funeral. That is agape love, a self-sacrificing act, not self-centered or self-preserving.

You can have the same relationship with Jesus Christ if you call upon His name. He is the great Savior. He will never leave you! Phileo love is a brotherly love, and it is a love that Jesus showed the apostles. He shared His life with them. When two men of faith share their dreams of meeting that special woman and enjoying a marriage fatherhood and brotherly companionship, they help each other to be the best husband, father, and friend they can be. When a brother in Christ is struggling with a problem, he can reach out to brother believers. Men of faith stand together for each other. We are not alone. You will not find the same friendship outside of God. Men who pursue self-pleasure and achievement through the world cannot be trusted to have the same relationship that men of God have. They do not strive to please the Lord, only their own pleasures and ulterior motives. Even godly men have to keep themselves accountable to God and fellow believers to make sure their helping hand is out of servanthood and not self-motivated.

A husband and wife share agape love, the sacrificial form of love serving each other without expectation or return. They share phileo love that brings them together first as friends, and then it grows to companionship. They share all that God has provided in their life. Their agape and phileo love, along with God's love for their marriage, keeps them bonded and secured when an intruder threatens their holy matrimony. Eros love brings husband and wife together physically. It is a physical love expression between a man and a woman, but it does not last. Eros love is fleeting, but God's sacrificial love saves them and bonds them when problems come crashing in. When a couple calls upon Jesus Christ in their crisis, He will not leave them behind. He will carry them through their trials.

Jesus will lead all of us who follow Him to the Promised Land. Christ put His wisdom and action together. Not only did he say the word, He put action to His word. That's what faith is about.

Why are so many Christians hypocrites? It is because we all have a fallen nature. The convicting word of God and other believers knock some of us off our holier-than-thou pedestal. In my opinion, hypocrisy stems from self-pride, and we constantly battle with our own vanity. We are to put God's words to our actions in order to glorify God and shine His light into darkness, not to glorify ourselves. We joyfully proclaim to others what Christ has done for us and what the Lord can do for others in need.

I continue to study Jesus, and I have discovered His characteristics I never knew before. Any man can relate to his ruggedness as a carpenter. The miles of road He traveled tells me He was an explorer searching for new lands and people to serve. Every region he went to, He reached out with open arms to bring wisdom and healing. The Bible describes Him as well versed in the Word of God because He is the Word. And yet He spoke out in love, not of law. Self-ego did not box him in; nor did He get caught in the euphoria of title before His name, like man does. His ultimate title became Lord and Savior. He paid a price He Himself did not owe but one we owed and could not pay on our own merit.

There are people who don't know the life of Jesus and how close He came to us while walking amongst us. Although many people believe in Jesus Christ, they don't believe they understand how they can have a personal relationship with someone who existed in ancient days gone by. After writing that latter sentence, many readers may ask, "How can I talk to a man I cannot see?"

Children have an innocence and an abundant belief because they don't expect anyone to lie to them. But as adults, we succumb to sin, and we are exposed to lies passed down through the ages. So we therefore hold skepticism and disbelief in every area of our life. We believe the lies of men with no reverence to God and deny divine truth. Unless we look at the world through childlike eyes, we will never see the fingerprint of God evident on the planet we live. I'd rather take a chance on a man I cannot see, but I have read His truth. I have never seen Christ with my own eyes, but I can tell you without a doubt that His presence surrounds me.

Sometimes the truth hurts. That's why we deny it, and God is very truthful with us in His Word, but he also gave us one great solution to the problems our sin has created. Now that's a loving God.

We were never meant to go our own way, our destiny through our good works. We do good works to give Him the glory. The Word of God is to guide us so our blessings can be shared, lest we boast in our own vanity. Again, we have choices. We can pursue what pleases us and never be happy or fulfilled.

Or we can please God in everything we do and receive His joy. When we open our hearts to His truth, then we will see the evidence of God the Father.

In my years of working for a civil service department serving the public, I have met people from all walks of life and many professions. I have engaged in conversation with many fine citizens of small-town warmth and hospitality, the kind of folks you would meet at the local coffee shop—from the bus driver to the package delivery person and from the garbage collector to the landscaper and oil delivery men. Men and women who work on the roadways and highways in various forms of employment share a bond. We may not perform the same work, but we interact with an inconsiderate public who either don't understand or just don't care about our duty, only that we seem to be in "their way."

Whatever work you perform is important to a civil society. A bus driver needs to safely drive a school bus and be of good character. Would any parent want a pervert transporting their schoolchildren? Garbage collectors help homes and streets by removing rotting refuse that causes disease. Men deliver heating oil and repair boilers so a family can sleep warm at night. The package deliverymen and women are under stressful timing to get their route complete on time, delivering not only personal items but lifesaving items to hospitals and vital documents to doctors. The landscaper is trying to maneuver through busy roadways with his or her equipment, struggling to keep his or her entrepreneurial business thriving and keeping his or her customers satisfied.

Highway workers relate to all of these people. We all share the road with distracted, obnoxious drivers whose only concern is their own agenda, and that selfish agenda often leads to the unnecessary harm of another person. When snow starts covering streets and highways during the winters of the Northeast, all of these people who we interact with on a daily basis are delighted to see the men and women who operate snow removal equipment in the public works department.

I have taken on various positions as traffic controller, and I have worked along with garbagemen, oftentimes assisting them with garbage cans, directing them around our equipment and guiding them in their vehicles while they maneuver their rigs through narrow work zones. These men perform their laborious and malodorous task with pride and valor. I admire them because of their unpretentious nature.

I have also interacted with many school bus drivers, and they are relieved to see our crews plowing streets in the winter and repairing roads that they travel daily on their bus route. School bus drivers know they are in good hands when they see our crews making the road as safe as possible, ensuring public safety on ice- and snow-covered streets.

One school morning in the winter, a bus driver let me out while I was waiting to exit the highway yard. And when I drove past her, she gave me two thumbs way up. It was an awesome feeling of encouragement to know that someone in this cruel, thoughtless world cares about the job you are doing. I don't know if this woman were a Christian, but I do know that she added sunshine to my dreary, snowy workday.

How about you, believer? Have you given someone a thumbs-up today? Have you lifted the spirits of anyone with your encouraging, Christ-influenced attitude? Have you offered a cup of coffee to someone whose occupation is to battle the elements of nature? Have you offered a bite to eat and an inspiring word to someone in the fierce and frantic corporate business world? Have you inspired a man to be a great man of God, a loving father to his children, and a nurturing husband to his wife? Have you encouraged a mother who is sacrificing to stay home and homeschool her children God's way through biblical education versus a godless world education in evolution? Or have you left someone with the sensation like he or she just had a tornado rip through his or her day? Now, believer, is the time to step up to the plate. Show who we are through acts of love and kindness and to God be the glory!

We who claim to be Christians have Christ in our name and should have Christ in our heart. We should be carrying the joy of the Lord with us. We are the only messengers of hope who are available to bring salt and light to a person's otherwise dark, lonely, and bitter world. We must constantly keep our actions in check and think how we will affect the next person to meet us.

Have you ever had someone in front of you when you are leaving a store and, as you approach the glass door, the person does not look behind him or her and the door slams you in the face? Our actions affect the people around us. Has common courtesy vanished along with chivalry? Well, I hope that person who let the door slam wasn't a believer, and if he or she were, I hope he or she reads this book.

Our actions tell people who we really are. Our hands should be reaching out to love and serve people. We should be available to offer hands-on prayer to the lost and hurting people around us. When the opportunity presents itself, we can witness God's love. We should be ready to offer encouraging and inspiring words to those who are discouraged in life. We want to be effective witnesses for Christ. But how can we do that when we don't follow through with His instruction from the Bible? We need Bible study to live a lifestyle of commitment, and we need to follow through as prayer warriors until the doors of heaven open and a person's cup overflows with God's grace.

Jesus showed us the way to have a beautiful life through Him. Our faith is a lifestyle. Is our conduct in public the same as what we do when no one else is watching us? We have the promise of eternal life through the sacrifice of our savior from what He did for us, not because of what we have done.

In my observation, it seems that some Christians take to their faith like a drink of water. Some take a full glass of water, and they are fully hydrated. Others take their glass half full, and they are partially hydrated. There are believers with a full glass of spirituality and those with a half glass. The full-glass believer spills over onto other people, while the half-glass believer does not spill over at all. I have known some believers who carry anger, resentment, and unforgiveness.

I know a person who acknowledges her faith; however, observing her actions leaves one with a cloud of doubt to this claim. I will call her "Sara." She has expressed bitterness and unforgiveness toward individuals in her life. It appears that God took away some people very dear to her life, and she holds anger and resentment toward others. Maybe instead of being angry at God, it is easier to hold a grudge against other believers or people. Only a professional explains why this behavior exists.

Why does God seem to take away certain loved ones from us? I do not have an answer to this question. But I do know the promise that God has for us who believe in Him, and He talks to us through His Word. If only we open our hearts, he will speak to us in His way. Even though Sara seems to carry the burden of anger and resentment, she still attends church, which sounds strange, but many angry and bitter people still do the same thing. Anger is a normal human response; however, if a person does not seek forgiveness, that anger turns into danger, both physically and mentally.

After observing Sara's behavior, I examined my own heart and asked myself, "Have I truly and honestly given all the mental and spiritual garbage of my past to God? Or am I still holding on to it? Is God the focus of my mind?"

Every believer must ask himself or herself this question. If our mind is focused on ourselves or our past mistakes that God has forgiven and Christ has cleansed us from, we cannot serve effectively. Perhaps to be seen in church feeds this self-focus and gives some people personal gratification of doing a good deed. The purpose of church assembly is to glorify God and to be in His presence. To read and follow His Word, not to show our good works. Some believers, even though they accepted Christ, are inclined to resolutely hold on to the pain and heartache of their past. It is a human problem. All Christians struggle with our human condition. Our self-character constantly battles with our new creation in Christ. We are righteous in Christ, not in our own selves.

In order to understand what the believing life is all about, I would recommend reading and studying the New Testament where Jesus instructs not only His disciples but future disciples, men and women. And that includes us today. The books of Matthew, Mark, Luke, and John are of benefit to start with. They describe the life of Jesus, along with the kind of life He called His followers to live.

A Christian is a forgiven sinner. We still sin because of our fallen nature, but we sin less. Our purpose in life is to please God. We live for Christ, and we glorify Him in the way we live. We desire to have less sin in our lives. We live with sin daily;

however, when we choose to live for Christ, our sin does not control us. We make a choice to live for sin or Christ. We need to focus on the character of Christ as the Bible describes. We need to take some time and pray daily. Every day, I ask the Lord in prayer to help me be an effective witness for Christ and to make a difference in someone's life. I need to forget myself and focus on the spiritual needs of others.

The Scripture tells me that God will take care of me, just as He takes care of the animals of the wild. If He provides food and shelter for the birds of the air, how much more will He take care of us? Allow Christ's holy spirit to clean your heart so the Lord can reside within you. Only He can remove that which clutters your heart and steals your joy. Remember, believers, everyone who meets you is witnessing Christ in you for the first time. If you are spiritually on fire for Jesus, His light will shine in you, and your salt will add flavor to that person you meet. Others around you will experience the agape love of Jesus Christ!

I strongly encourage you to read and study the New Testament account of Jesus in Matthew, Mark, Luke, and John. These books in the Bible describe Jesus Christ so you can know Him personally, who He was, and why He existed. Try to study the actions of Christ. His acts are very important to read because a believer is electively called to carry on His acts of love. We must have a willing and available heart to serve Him and to live out the servanthood that Jesus began. The only way a person will know Jesus Christ the Son and God our heavenly Father is through those who allow the light and Word of Jesus Christ to shine through them and into the lives of others who only know darkness.

Chapter 3

Is God in Your Marriage?

It all starts with a boy who has a crush on a girl. That boy grows into a man who does not want to be alone. He desires a woman to decorate his life. He longs for one woman who brings beauty and color to his otherwise drab life without changing who he is. In return, the woman receives a companion and lifelong friend. If a man is raised in God's principles, he learns to live to serve others, and the wife has a husband after God's own heart. However, if he lives by his own self-seeking desires, chances are, he may fail as a spouse. I know. I have been there.

Living by biblical instruction does not mean living by religious rules and regulations. It requires loving selflessly and giving to people in need whether we like them or not because they are children of God. These principles are defined as giving without expectation of receiving. When we love someone by giving our time, we fill that person with the love of God. When we give so much of ourselves, it overflows in that person that he or she is receiving the joy that someone else gave us through his or her sacrifice. God created woman so man would not be alone. Companionship is marriage, and God is the author. And He does not make mistakes. "Oops" is not in God's vocabulary. The problem is an imperfect man marrying an imperfect woman.

Marriage is about servanthood, and this part of marriage has been completely distorted. The husband and wife are equal in serving each other. God did not create man as the king of the household and the wife as the doormat. He created companionship, the husband and wife serving each other without any expectation of return. When you love your spouse, you are loving God because your spouse is a child of God.

Most marriages take place in a church or similar faith-based setting. But once the ceremony is over, that's it. The couple is on its own to take on the trials of life. Marriage is a personal and spiritual commitment that a man and woman make together. This institution founded by a loving Creator consists of a three-strand cord: God the Father, the husband, and the wife. No one can break this strong cord as long as it is kept together yoked in faith. Spouses united in faith together can withstand the storms of marriage, and they can protect themselves from the enemy of marriage, but this is only possible through the Lord. It would make sense that man would take seriously an institution created by God so man would not be alone. But if God is not in our minds, we are open to believe the darkest lie. When God is not in our mind, what looks attractive and fulfilling deceives us. If what we desire does not come from God, it is a poisonous lie.

A man of God is willing and available to do whatever it takes by God's command to make his marriage work. His wife must be yoked in unity with him. However in order for a man to take his stand to protect his marriage, he must know what the handbook of marriage says, and that book is the Bible. Any marriage that does not consistently adhere to the biblical principles of marriage is headed for disaster. Marriage is about serving without expecting anything in return. Sadly, many marriages ceremonies are performed at the altar and may eventually end sometime thereafter.

Once the bride and groom leave the altar, they are subject to the influence of negative worldly views toward marriage. Why is it that, once the newlyweds leave the altar, they are on their own to figure out married life? Most couples get married in church and have a traditional ceremony. But marriage is more than tradition, and ceremony is it not. A husband and wife companionship with God with the help and support of the church is a way of an abundant relationship.

Are churches putting too much focus on tithing and building bigger churches instead of helping to build better marriages and defending them? Shouldn't the church, the body of believers, have some responsibility to help husbands and wives build a strong marriage and defend it against the ungodliness of the world? Think about this. Professional careers and marriage are similar in nature, are they not? You need schooling to be a professional (doctor, police officer, or firefighter), and even after schooling and training, these professionals continue to receive more so they are prepared to manage life's constant and ever-changing problems.

Even an effective teacher of the gospel needs continual training and study to be in the Word of God. Why should marriage be viewed any differently? Motherhood is a career. And how can you have a church when you don't have families? If it weren't for wives and mothers, there would be no churches. The holy Word of God is where marriage is found. In the New Testament, Jesus set the standard of God's principles through His apostles, and in those verses is where you will discover God's word on marriage.

"Love is not rude, it is not self-seeking, it is not easily angered, it keeps no record of wrongs" (1 Cor. 13:5). Love flows through a marriage that lives up to mutual responsibility. God created marriage so man would have a companion. A husband and wife raise children in a household who serves the Lord. The focus of marriage is being helpmates to each other. A husband and wife tend to each other's needs without expectation of reward. That is agape love. When you serve your spouse, you are loving God, and you are blessed. A blessing is an unexpected gift from God. A reward is an expected gift that man constantly pursues.

The Bible reveals the principles of marriage to those who open this Word of God. You give actions of help to your spouse out of a joyous attitude, not a "do for me and I'll do for you" approach. A husband and wife who live to please God in their marriage embody prayer and Scripture reading. But a marriage without God and prayer is open to self-pride, anger, and unforgiveness, leaving both spouses lonely and abandoned.

Though you were marrying your best friend and lifelong mate, somewhere something went wrong. A change occurred, and the relationship became self-centered and one-sided instead of serving one another as if serving God himself, which is what spouses are doing for each other. Marriage is a perfect institution that God authorized and founded. The problem is an imperfect man marrying an imperfect woman. Remember the Bible tells us that relationships started with Adam and Eve. God designed men and woman to be different but also to rely on each other. A husband and wife are to complement each other. God designed man to be the protector and provider. He designed woman to be the homemaker and teacher. Society has reversed these roles, and now the term "homemaker" is degrading to women.

When the roles of husband and wife work together, families are bonded in love and service to God. When a husband and wife work against each other or reverse family roles, chaos and confusion erupts, dividing that family.

A couple needs God in their marriage for the reason that He created this union, so it will not work without Him. He made us to depend on one another and to rely on Him. Only God can provide our needs, and we were created to serve one another. God created the marriage companionship. If God is removed, spouses will have trouble they alone cannot remedy or control. Marriage creates the best environment for raising children.

I know of some moms who homeschool their children. Although homeschool moms face difficulty, their children are receiving a creation education and respect for humanity. These children are also taught to honor their parents and to respect authority, and they are being taught biblical life lessons. These life instructions are not being taught in public schools. In public schools, the Bible and prayer have been removed and replaced with violence, bullying, and a lack of respect for humanity. Many school systems are replacing creation education with evolution education and teaching anti-capitalism. In homeschooling, a mother has the freedom to teach her children the elementary basics and include biblical education, whereas outside the family, home, God, and government are being separated.

Before discussing marriage further, I would like to touch on some concerns for men and women considering marriage during courtship. This concern is personality adjustment. Some people are quite well adjusted in their behavior, while others are not. Most serious relationship problems arise when one or both partners have some long-standing problematic personality characteristics. Once we marry these problems, in some cases, behavior disorders are even more likely to be triggered because of the new levels of intimacy, responsibility, and adjusting to living together required in marriage. When courting someone, we should be aware of these behaviors. It is also important to be with a person who shares the same faith and is willing to receive counseling and guidance if these behaviors exist.

A courtship period is a preferred resolve to discovering these behaviors. A courtship time can be up to two years, but having patience is a virtue that will save a man and woman from making a wrong choice.

A description of an emotionally well-adjusted person would look something like this:

Healthy behavior	Unhealthy behavior
Composed	Highly anxious
Happy	Depressed
Optimistic	Negative and pessimistic
Realistic	Unrealistic
Respectful	Disrespectful
Able to communicate	Hidden
Sympathetic and caring	Unsympathetic
Sensitive to others	Insensitive
Self aware and open	Defensive
Objective	Subjective
Flexible	Rigid and controlled
Patient	Impatient
Amiable	Hostile
Humble	Proud
Thoughtful	Impulsive
Good self esteem	Low self esteem
Honest and direct	Manipulative

Open to others	Closed and hidden
Secure	Insecure
Assertive without being domineering and controlling	Control by aggression

This is just an idea of some behaviors that could present a problem in a relationship. One should use practical judgment, for example, with being happy. We may not physically express happiness twenty-four hours a day. Happiness and joy can fill us even if we are not showing it in our body language. There will be times when we will show unhappiness, sadness, and grief. However, there may be underlying behavior problems if a person remains in that state for a prolonged period of time. As believers, we are to be filled with the joy of the Lord after our period of grieving. "There is a time to weep and a time to laugh, a time to mourn and a time to dance" (Eccl. 3:4).

Another behavior situation is a mate who is subjective and bears hidden prejudice toward the other mate versus an objective spouse who is open to discussion on important family matters such as finance. Events in our life affect our emotional behaviors. Experiencing them is healthy, but to stay in these behaviors and not receive the joy of the Lord is unhealthy.

So how does a husband and wife have a healthy marriage? God created this companionship; therefore, only He can keep a husband and wife together who are both yoked in their faith. However, both spouses have to forsake all others and focus on God in their marriage. God is the glue in your marriage. He creates a strong bond in your relationship that no one can break unless the husband and wife allow it. Some men take the wrong view of marriage, and they distort the Scripture in their own mind.

> Wives, submit to your husbands as to the Lord. For the husband is the head of the wife as Christ is the head of the church, His body, of which He is the Savior. Now as the church submits to Christ, so also wives should submit to their husband in everything (Eph. 5:22–24).

This verse has been abused for one's own purpose to control his wife, and because of this, women hold much animosity toward it because of that distortion. Do we truly understand what God is telling husbands in this passage? The apostle Paul devotes twice as many words to instructing men to love their wives as to instructing wives to submit to their husbands. How should a man love his wife? He should be willing to sacrifice everything for her. He should put her well-being in a place of primary importance. He should care for her as he cares for his own body. No wife should fear submitting to a man who cares for her in this way. God does not refer to a wife as a slave or servant to a husband's selfish whims. Matter of fact, this verse calls all men to be responsible in Christ for their wives. A wife is to submit to her husband's authority. God governs a husband's authority, making the husband a mutual servant. Are men of God loving their wife and home with God's sacrificial love? A wife is not material matter. She is flesh and blood, and a wife chooses to be with her husband because she believes he is the man for her and a man after God's heart. If that's the man you are, your wife will flourish because God is in you. But if you are self-seeking, your wife will wither away like an unloved and untended flower. To be godly is to let the love of God flow through you. The latter verse is not a license to beat, whip, or curse a wife into submission. By living under this commandment, a wife is submitting to her husband's authority to which

God has given to those who are men of God. God calls men who are after His heart.

> Husbands, love your wives, just as Christ loved the church and gave Himself up for her to make her holy, cleansing her by the washing with through the word, and to present her to Himself as a radiant church, without stain or wrinkle or any other blemish, but holy and blameless (Eph. 5:25–26).

Believers are the church; therefore, Christ sacrificed Himself for an imperfect body of believers. Men of God are to protect and nourish their wife and to sacrificially love her, and that is defined as putting her needs before self-needs. We must be careful with this verse because it has been distorted and twisted to make it sound like a husband is a god over his wife. A husband is not a god over his wife. He is a servant of love, forgiveness, and compassion to his wife. He serves his wife out of love without expectation. A husband is not to take the king role and rule his wife and family with an iron fist. That is not God's way for marriage. There should be only one king in your household, and His name is Jesus. The husband is to dedicate his home to God's Word and direction. "As for my house we will serve the Lord" (Josh. 24:15).

It is so important in a Christian marriage that two believers are yoked together. Spiritual congruency is of the utmost importance. Husband and wife are servants to each other. They nourish each other, and that is God's greater plan. Problems arise when a couple drifts away from God. The three cord frays, breaks away from God, and becomes two separate cords. When that happens, ungodly influences enter the marriage.

The world has a plethora of answers as to how couples can solve their problems. The world has conjured solutions and advice found in counselors of worldly philosophy and alternatives. Husbands and wives are convinced with false evidence that marriage can work without God. How can marriage work any other way than from the master plan and the one who wrote it?

Let's take another look at the latter verse, Ephesians 5:22. This verse is intended for a godly husband to lead his wife as God leads the husband. A husband is to lead his wife in a godly, loving way, not strong-arming her. Marriage is a safe haven for husband and wife. It is not a prison sentence. This verse does not indicate that the wife is weak-minded; neither is she a slave to her husband. Matter of fact, this verse places responsibility on the husband to direct his wife just as Christ loves and directs the church through His Holy Spirit. Just as a body of believers loves each other in Christ, so does a husband love his wife. Jesus gives direction to the body of believers through the Word of God in truth and love. So be it that the husband, a servant himself, leads his wife and family through the truth and love of the Word of God. A husband who is a man of God leads his wife and family by his own example.

I have listened to accounts of husbands abusing their wives, both mentally and physically, in the name of religion. My mother shared with me what she learned about this in a Bible study group. She called it "domination in the guise of service." The Bible describes God as our Creator overflowing with agape love without end, compassionate and forgiving. Husbands who abuse their wives are not men after God's heart; neither do they honor God. A husband who lives by God's principles nurtures his wife, children, and family. A man of God does not rule his wife or his family like a despot. He loves and nurtures his spouse and children because that's what God commands and that is God's nature.

The husband is to serve his wife in prayer and fellowship with other believing couples. He is to love and protect his wife and children, both physically and mentally. That's why it is so important for believers to wait on the will of God. Just as He brought Eve to Adam in the garden, he will bring a man to his wife. God will also bring a woman to her husband. As long as this union is the will of God, the two will be yoked together in faith. But if we succumb to our loneliness and disregard patience, we will open ourselves to relationships that are not the will of God and potentially harmful and toxic to us. A strong marriage requires a husband and wife who are equally joined and bonded in faith.

Marriage starts with the man because God created him first. Just as God saw the first man tending the garden alone, He also sees all men who are alone. Those who are in His plan to be with a companion, he places such a mate. God pours out His sanctified and sacrificial love on men abundantly for those who receive Him. So should a man of God pour out his sanctified and sacrificial love for the woman he loves. A husband's duties are protection, provision, honor, and service of her needs.

Perhaps the reason for many affairs is because the boyfriend is willing to do for his mistress what her husband has given up on. Marriage is not for controlling and dictating. Here again I mention the latter verse from Ephesians 5:22 because it is extremely important to understand what it does and does not say. A woman is to submit to her godly husband, and the key word is "godly," to be a man of God. The next verse instructs a husband to love his wife just as Christ Himself loved the church and gave Himself for her. This verse is either overlooked or ignored. A godly husband thrives on his wife's respect, but that respect is earned, not demanded, from his wife. If your spouse is in your life at God's will, she will respond to your unconditional love and respect you in return.

Husbands should study this verse, as it will help in your marriage, along with hands-on prayer with your spouse. The choice for a healthy marriage is mutual between husband and wife. Husbands and wives praying together for each other's needs is the most intimate act of love you can perform. For a husband, it is the most masculine practice you do for your spouse, to pray that the Lord our God would guard your wife's heart and eyes and to give her a joyful spirit. This daily act of love signifies the utmost expression of your love for your wife! Wives, I encourage you to practice this lifestyle.

Also, this act of love is powerful and declares your love for him. I wish my heart were ready to receive this when I married. Well, it is not too late for me, and neither is it too late for you.

If you are not in a relationship right now, you must do something for yourself and make it a daily part of your life. Don't do this in haste. Give yourself time, find a quiet place somewhere, and focus on your situation. How important is it for you to have a companion to share your life with? Our flesh wants anybody, but our hearts are made of glass and easily broken. Do you want to make that delicate choice yourself, or will you trust in God to make that decision for you? Will you trust and wait upon God to bring your life mate who will hold your glass heart in his or her gentle hands? Let God make the decision who will be in your life.

To love God is to love people. You must love God if you are going to give yourself to others, and that also works in marriage. To love others is to love and please God. If you don't love God first, you will not love anyone else. You will only have a self-focus in your heart of who can please you. Love God first, and you can love anyone with agape love. If you are looking for someone special in your life, you need to pray to your heavenly Father. In His eyes and His heart, you are His child. Ask in prayer for a life companion, someone who shares your faith and loves God as much as you do. Pray for the patience to wait until God brings that person into your life. Make this daily devotion a lifestyle. If you want a companion who walks and talks with you and accepts you in all your strengths and weaknesses, then you need to take heed to this advice. You will reap the fruit of your answered prayers in a spouse whom God has chosen for you, and God does not make mistakes.

I am an avid listener to Christian radio. My station broadcasts a program called "Focus on the Family." One day, the topic was a guest pastor discussing the talk he had with his daughter's prom date, and the issue was on raising young men of God. I can't remember it verbatim, but the point of the topic left an indelible impression in my mind since that day I heard it a few years ago. This youth minister recalled a conversation he had with his daughter's prom date. The young man arrived on time, and the father welcomed the teen suitor dressed neatly in a tuxedo and offered a seat while waiting for his princess in a prom dress to greet him. The conversation the father was about to have with this young gentleman was not the typical "you have her back before midnight, or you'll answer to my Winchester!" warning speech. No, this was a father talking to his daughter's prom date. The father began to counsel to the young man what the father's responsibilities for his daughter were. The father showed honor and dignity to his daughter. He protected her body from harm and her purity from immorality. He was to ensure that she enjoyed life without any regrets morally and remained chaste until marriage. The father expressed to the young man that, when he took his prom date to the prom, he was now taking on the same role of responsibility the father had taken. The father did not expect this lad to be perfect, but he did presume him to show respect, dignity, and chivalry to his daughter and to enjoy the evening without any guilt or regret of their actions.

I don't know whatever became of that young man. I did weep after listening to this moving interview with the pastor and father. I did not go to my high school prom, but I did take my girlfriend who was five years my junior to her prom. I remember that night, and although no backseat acts of passion took place in our limousine, I wasn't a perfect gentleman either, maybe by religious and social standards but not by biblical standards. I certainly did not get that life-changing talk with a father or youth pastor that the young man in the radio program received. No man gave me a speech like that. No men of virtuous influence were in my life at that time.

I think about the opportunity that opened for that young lad when he heard that life talk from a loving, caring dad who walked with God. What if a man had given me a life-changing conversation like the latter one when I was in my adolescence? I was very impressionable, and I truly believe a heart-to-heart talk like that would have given me a different perspective on living a life being a responsible man to a woman. We need men of God who want to live for God and please Him in their lives, to glorify Him and care for women the way God wants us to care for them for who they are, children of God.

If we do not have God on our mind, the world's school of

toxic and "stinking" thinking fill us. We get a dishonorable degree in mistreating women. Thoughts become action and can eventually turn into perverse and vile physical actions and mental abuse.

I often wonder what my life would be like if I had men of God as role models in my youth to show me what it means to be a man of faith and ethical conduct. Maybe I would have been able to be the husband my wife needed and I wouldn't have two broken marriages. Husbands and dads, you can change your family's life so they have a better future. Bring your family to church. Husband and wife, get together and get involved in Bible study. Churches, get ready to be involved in bringing families together. If the body of believers don't take action to save God's family, who will?

Any man can father a child, but a family needs a husband, a dad who is willing to try his best to live a life of virtue and have a heart for God. Of course, a man may fall. After all, we are fallible, but a supportive family will pick him up and cheer him on to be the best man of God he can be. A wife needs a husband who listens with patience and understanding. He doesn't have to fix the problem. Just listen. A husband needs a wife who respects him and catches him when he fails after trying to be a leader for his family. A sports team needs their fans and cheering squad to inspire them to win a victory. A husband needs his wife's support and cheerleading to conquer the giants in his life and be victorious. A family needs a husband/father who honors, respects, and conducts order in his home without being physically or verbally abusive. A father needs to correct a child's bad behavior and not show the kind of discipline from a father with personal anger issues. A family needs a father who is a role model for the kind of man a daughter seeks to find in her adult life. A family needs the kind of father who is raising a young boy into a man of faith, honor, and civil and moral conduct. Adolescent boys require an involved dad who will raise honorable young men of God.

The negativity I hear about born-again Christians really disturbs me. What possibilities would I have throughout my life to serve people other than myself if my heart were open to the Good News a Christian had shared with me back then? Perhaps I would not have been so reckless and careless about other people in word and in action. Maybe I could have had a chance at a long-standing marital companionship instead of two broken ones.

The institution of marriage has a spiritual enemy and must be defended. In the garden, the serpent came upon Eve and gave her a lie with the fruit of knowledge from the tree of life. Those same lies exist today that try to pry couples away from each other. That's why a husband and wife must study the Bible, for there is power in the Word of God. Only the powerful Word of God can protect spouses from lies that threaten their marriage. The only way for a couple bonded in faith to defend their marriage from ungodly influences is to devote each other to a lifestyle of prayer and Scripture reading. Daily devotional Scripture reading and hands-on prayer greatly increases recovery in difficult times. A husband and wife who do not maintain a godly marital foundation will eventually find themselves in a war of blame, bitterness, self-pride, and treachery. Neither spouse will admit either is wrong. Rather than confessing their own faults, everyone else is to blame for the problem or conflict. A marriage with both spouses battling for self-rights becomes a no-win situation that leads to the legal war zone of divorce court. A spouse admitting he or she is wrong does not indicate that he or she is weak. The Bible says that love does not keep a record of mistakes. A spouse who lives by the Word doesn't remember the other spouse's mistakes. The more we learn from our mistakes, the stronger and wiser we become.

A husband and wife joined together by God can work out differences and difficulties when perilous times strike in a marriage. Communication, cooperation, and prayer, along with fellowship with other believing husbands and wives, will keep the marriage strong. Marriage counseling through the church can also be of great benefit and support. A husband and wife who share conservative beliefs will have less conflict in their marriage due in part to their congruent beliefs and views on building a family and raising children. A believing couple strives harder to commit to each other and to glorify God in their marriage.

Suppose a man and woman enter a marriage where they have opposing viewpoints regarding family and child rearing. These conflicts may intensify on social and political issues that affect matter of family and faith. They may even disagree with each other on the Bible if it is not a marriage built on faith. Issues such as different taste in foods, weather climates, and shopping preferences are trivial and should not be the deal breaker to a marriage. But it is a crucial situation when one spouse opposes the other over important matter such as handling family finances, raising children in the Word of God, and opposing each other on biblical truths. This will make a turbulent relationship.

Remember, marriage is companionship. This has been stated before, but it is very true. God saw that man was alone and said it was not good for man to be that way, so He created woman as a companion for the man. It seems that many new

Christians think that, as long as they believe in God and Jesus and attend church, they don't have to read or study the Bible other than church. The Bible is a shield of truth. Not staying in the Word of God is like a police officer without his or her protective vests, a soldier without an armored vehicle in fierce battle, or a firefighter entering a blazing room without his or her hose line. Our Bibles are our shields against spiritual attacks. In our walk of faith, Jesus and the Bible go together like bread and water. We must eat and drink to sustain our physical life. We need Christ and the Word of God to sustain our spiritual life.

Many couples, young and old, will enter holy matrimony without understanding what the Bible teaches about a fruitful bond in God's love. We live in a disposable society, and sadly, God's creation of marriage is being tossed to the curb for morning refuse collection. We are not waste for someone's temporary and disposable pleasures. We are human beings. We need to cherish other people because we are all children of God, who is loving, forgiving, and protective. What we do to other people, good or bad, we are also doing to God. We are made in our heavenly Father's image. "So God created man in His own image, in the image of God He created him; male and female He created them" (Gen. 1:27).

A husband and wife can prevent their marriage from destruction, but remember this takes a husband and wife who are willing to keep God in their marriage. "Though one may be overpowered, two can defend themselves. A cord of three is not easily broken" (Eccl. 4:12). I heartily beseech couples who are marriage bound to attend a church that teaches Bible study and champions the message of eternal salvation through Jesus Christ.

It is important to read and study the New Testament

verses on marriage. One of these talks about submission is in 1 Corinthians 11:3. "The head of every man is Christ, and the head of the woman is man, and the head of Christ is God." Submission is a key element in the smooth functioning of any business, government, or family. God ordained submission in certain relationships to prevent chaos. It is essential to understand that submission is not surrender, withdrawal, or apathy. It does not mean inferiority because God created all people in His image and all have equal value. Submission is mutual commitment and cooperation. Thus, God calls for submission among equals. He did not make the man superior. He made a way for man and woman to work together. Jesus Christ, although equal with God the Father, submitted to Him to carry out the plan for salvation. Likewise, although equal to man under God, the wife should submit to her husband for the sake of their marriage and family. Submission between equals is submission by choice, not force. We serve God in these relationships by willingly submitting to others in our church and to our spouses.

Some areas in our life need preparation. We prepare for school by doing our homework. Marriage is no different, and there is so much to learn about the why, when, and where marriage came from.

But mankind turned marriage into a family tradition and perhaps a rite of passage for a boy to become a man. But that is not why God created marriage. Therefore, if we want to know why marriage exists, we must go and study the book that teaches and instructs on marriage. Companionship is a very close friendship between a husband and wife, and both serve each other because they want to, not because they have to. If a man and woman are not ready for this relationship of sacrificing, serving, and loving unconditionally, no matter what life throws at the two until death do they part, they have much to contemplate.

Before you reach that altar, think about the latter sentence. If either is not ready, it is better to rescind your decision to marry before you reach the altar. Yes, a heart may be broken, but the power of Jesus Christ can heal our heart. I believe it is better to suffer a broken heart than to make a lifelong vow with someone than to become antagonists trapped for life. Is there a way to avoid marrying the wrong person? Yes, I have learned this lesson through the Bible after graduating from the school of hard knocks. God is all knowing and omnipresent. He created man; therefore, He knows what our needs are. He observed Adam in the garden alone and said it was not good, so He created the woman for companionship.

I always went looking for my mate before I read the Bible, and of course, I erred because I wasn't really looking for a friend or companion. I have learned from the Word of God that companionship is a gift from God. I always searched for the gift when I discovered through the Word that God has my gift, my companion, waiting for me. A gift arrives when you least expect it, so when we pray and ask God for that companionship, we must wait patiently, just as we wait for our birthday to receive a gift. My advice to those of you seeking a relationship is to let God do the work. Let Him search for your mate, your lifelong companion. He knows us better than we know ourselves.

If you are married or if you have hopes of being married, this discussion is for you. Prayer makes for a strong marriage. Practice this action of hands-on praying with your future spouse. It is the second-most intimate act you can do with your beloved.

If you have never done this before, it may feel awkward

and uncomfortable in the beginning, but once you make it a lifestyle, the results are inspiring. Trust in the Lord that this act will save your marriage from destructive forces that want to leave both of you alone and bitter. This is a serious act of love, and you are protecting and preparing your spouse for the world he or she is going to walk through for the day. By praying over your mate, you are asking the Lord's Holy Spirit to do what you cannot do. Forget your feelings and pride. These self-emotions will not help you protect your relationship. A man and woman need to get out of their comfort zone and begin to spiritually protect their marriage. This is also another act of love.

What is hands-on praying for your spouse or intended? Find a quiet place for a few precious moments. You gently place your hand upon your mate and pray a simple request in your own words for protection, provision, wisdom, and faithfulness. Ask your spouse/future spouse what other needs he or she has that you can pray for. This is not religion. This is a relationship with God to love your spouse and to communicate with each other and God. A husband and wife are supposed to have this relationship with their heavenly Father, the author of marriage. Some prayer suggestions are to give your spouse faithful eye, wise decisions, and godly choices and ask the Lord to guard both your hearts. Men, the enemy of marriage has a fiery arrow aimed and ready to burn your marriage. The best way to fireproof your marriage is to devote hands-on prayer time to each other and stay fervently in the word of God.

Ladies, in this chapter, I drilled the men on the importance of safeguarding your marriage through hands-on prayer and reading the Word of God without ceasing. I also stressed the importance of understanding the chapter from Ephesians about submission. I hopefully drove this message home to the hearts of men longing for a life companion and for good reason.

In my perspective, America has a problem with the American husband. The image of the husband and father has been painted (or tainted, I would say) as a foolish and ignorant man with no other value than to be a yes-man for everyone. With the help of the media, these insults and attacks have been intensified on the American husband and father.

Women are being convinced they don't need a man to raise a family. Men are succumbing to the pressure of this role reversal. There was a time in America when being a dad meant having purpose and significant positive influence. Sadly, this position does not hold the same stature today. Any man with functioning organs can be a father, but a dad takes his son fishing. He takes his son to the ball game and shows his son how to change the oil in his car. Dad is the role model in a young boy's life. He shows him how to treat women in a way that pleases God. Only a dad can take his daughter to the park and fly a kite. Only a dad can take his daughter out sleigh riding in the winter and end the day with a hot cup of chocolate. Dads, where are you?

We all have needs that only God can provide because we are all His creation. A woman needs a man who cares for her needs, nurtures her, and provides for her. Men are no longer of that nature today because society has weakened the man to depend on the woman. Women are being influenced that they don't need a man to help them and they can perform both roles. The united role of mom and dad created by God has been altered, and we are deceived that we have an alternative plan other than the original family plan that God set forth.

Today, society and media have painted a negative portrait of the American husband and dad. Today's dad is a dunce who his wife and his children place in his corner for a time-out when he is bad. That's why relationships need the truth of God's love through His Word for a solid marital foundation.

There is a problem with replacing husband and wife and mom and dad. Man will never replace what God created. Every problem we have is mankind working against God and pursuing our own interest. God's will is to see His children flourish. Men are struggling with a multitude of problems and getting no help from the media. Media messages, both audio and visual, that condone promiscuous and unfaithful behavior constantly bombard us. These messages of subliminal and literate become thought, and if this thought continues to grow, it may become an action.

Speaking of messages, an invention in our age began as a resource for entertainment and information. This electronic device has become quite influential in our homes. It has also gained much control over our lives and influenced our homes, families, and relationships. Spouses and children all across our land tune out their loved ones and tune into the god of invisible airwaves. The television launched family-friendly programming in its infancy. However today, an atmosphere that is not family friendly continues to grow, and families are divided. Is the influential power of television to blame? My mother has shared memories of listening to radio programs of the 1940s and 1950s. She recalls a variety of radio broadcasts, from young to old listener. Some very suspenseful programs thrilled listeners, but nothing was extremely violent or sexually suggestive. Today, a parent needs help with parental controls and even viewing what seems to be every movie to ensure it is child friendly and free of sexual innuendos, drugs, and alcohol content.

Ultimately, we have a choice where we want to focus our attention to. Objects like the television, telephone, and countless other devices have become gods in our lives and taken away our attention from the people we love. But we allowed this to happen to ourselves and our families. If we want to take back our relationship with our spouse, children, and parents, we have to go back to the basics.

But we are not perfect, and that is why we need God in our lives. God enables us to be the providers and nurturers that we were originally created to be, for husband and wife to be each other's companion and help mate. Husbands, don't you want to be your wife's hero, the only man she can rely on? Wives, don't you want to be the one he confides in and seeks advice without ridicule? The only way to be a man or woman of God is to study the Word of God together and surround yourselves with encouraging believers. Embrace each other in daily prayer time.

Maybe you're thinking to yourself, "That's a minister's job to pray over us."

Is anyone of you in trouble? He should pray. Is anyone happy? Let him sing songs of praise. Is anyone of you sick? He should call the elders of the church to pray over him and anoint him with oil in the name of the Lord. And the prayer offered in faith will make the sick person well; the Lord will raise him up. If he has sinned, he will be forgiven. Therefore confess your sins to each other and pray for each other so that you may be healed. The prayer of a righteous man is powerful and effective (James 5:13–16).

In this verse, being righteous means through the Lord and not within ourselves. Although this verse notes the prayer of a righteous man, it can also be addressed to women. The prayer of a righteous woman is powerful and effective. A child and a spouse need the prayer of a righteous mother and wife. Also, this verse does not imply that prayer should be limited to church leadership. Jesus proclaimed that we are to pray for one another. Husbands can and should pray over their spouses and children. Ladies, if your husband will succeed at striving to be the best husband and father, then you are his cheerleader. He needs your encouraging words. Your husband needs you to be honest with him without bringing him down to his knees with a criticizing comment. Wives, if you want your husband to win the game of life, he needs you and your family to cheer him on to the finish line.

Husbands, these encouraging and inspiring words work both ways. Remember how important your wife and family are to you, and they need to hear it and see your gratitude. We can bring God's family back, but we need to insist God stay in our marriage so all families can succeed in the name of Christ. Without almighty God, there are no great families, and with no great families, there is no great nation.

I have witnessed believing couples who have communication and companionship in their marriage. They are congruent in their faith and what the Bible says, and they are aware of social and political issues that affect marriage, families, and children. Do these couples disagree on anything? Yes, however, they don't allow these disagreements to become giants that can destroy their marriage. Some spouses who are opposites can give a relationship a unique and interesting flavor in a positive and constructive way.

What can be conflictive in a marriage is when a husband and wife oppose each other in marriage, family, child, and financial matters. Financial matters cause the most damage. Another dividing conflict is when spouses maintain opposing values, one conservative and the other not. This can cause extreme friction. When these two viewpoints clash, there will be division in the marriage and the family. The husband and wife both need to stand on rock-solid principles.

Before I received Christ as my Savior, I never knew couples whose marriage was established on biblical principles. Since my new life in Christ, I have met several couples who have a harmonious marriage based on the Word of God.

Pastor Tony and his wife have three girls who have grown into young adults raised on the Word of God. Pastor Tony has talked about marriage and difficulties that arise and how it is so important to be in the Word of God to carry you through the problems of life. He also emphasizes that it is important to praise God through our difficulties. Sometimes our quandaries are a necessary process to strengthen our character and to keep us close in our relationship with God.

Nick and his wife Andrea are friends of mine. They have four children, now grown men of God raised in a family of biblical instruction. They are also gifted musicians and burgeoning evangelists. Nick and Andrea are both involved in ministry. Nick guides husbands; Andrea helps women with godly direction. That's what our faith is about, reaching, teaching, and providing counsel in truth and love. Believing spouses help other couples who are confused and troubled, flopping around in life like a fish out of water looking for the quenching water of life. A husband and wife need spiritual water to sustain their relationship. I have noticed that, whatever Nick and Andrea do in service to the Lord, they do together as husband and wife. They are never really separate from another, maybe in distance at times but not in their relationship.

I have recently met another believing couple who put a light on another area of difference. Pastor Roberto leads a gathering of God's faithful, and his wife Amanda is also involved in women's ministry in the church. They have expressed disagreements in their relationship regarding individual appeals. They have compromised and managed to work out their troubles through prayer and communication with each other. A diversity in their marriage has surely worked in God's plan for them. Pastor Roberto is Hispanic; his wife is Caucasian. In God's eyes, unconditional love and companionship is all that matters.

In man's eyes, zebras should stick with zebras. Well, we are not wild animals. We are civilized human beings, creations of God. Mankind has opinions on what group of people should be together. But to God who had created us, unconditional love and shared faith is the factor in how a relationship will work, not the culture or background we come from. The women in these marriages live by biblical instruction that works in their relationship. They have trusted their husbands to God to be the man to take the lead in their marriage by faith, love, and respect. Most conservative women entrust their husbands to maintain the man role. Non-conservative women are inclined to lead their husbands and reverse the roles of husband and wife altogether. That is why a husband and wife must be yoked in faith and life through biblical instruction together.

I became a believer in the Word of God later in my life. These believing couples have become role models for me and given me hope that God will bring a woman of faith into my life to be my wife and life companion.

Relationships are about sacrifice for each other. That's how God made it because our sin causes us to dedicate ourselves to our won pleasure, and sacrificing our needs for our mate goes against our self-desires. Christ established the church as the embodiment of marriage. When a couple decides they want to get married, most give counsel to get married in a church. Because believers gathered together signify the church, shouldn't the body of believers be the ones to support and defend marriage and prevent divorce? Are engaged couples receiving marital instruction through the Word of God? Proper instruction can prevent potential marital disasters. What are churches doing to help couples prevent divorce? What programs are churches offering in marital education? The Bible provides our education on marriage, and every student needs to be educated before taking vows and entering into this lifelong commitment. Fellow husband and wife believers need to reach anyone seeking marriage who is not aware of this information, which is God's plan.

In my opinion, believers who stand for God's plan for marriage are responsible to reach out and invite couples to church and to show nonbelievers the church body is a family-friendly and family-defending institution that Christ Jesus established. Married couples can host a home Bible study on marital education in the Bible. If the body of believers does not take action in what Christ commanded to reach out and help husbands and wives in marital peril, then who else will rescue God's plan for marriage and families? Genesis 18:32 "Then he said, 'May the Lord not be angry, but let me speak just once more. What if only ten can be found there? He answered, "For the sake of ten, I will not destroy it." This verse speaks to all believers regarding where we stand for God. He loves us but do we love Him enough to stand up for what He created?

Are there ten righteous couples who will stand together for God's marriage plan? Christian husbands and wives have the opportunity to help marriages in trouble for God and to reach those who have not heard what God's plan is for their marriage and their lives.

The idea of having a relationship with a person while having no physical intimacy with him or her is antiquated and unrealistic to most people in today's modern age of relationships. How do we know if we can cohabitate as a couple without first sleeping together? A relationship takes more than eros love to survive. Only unconditional love will last through the crucial times of difficult economic periods and critical family and social issues. God's Word says that marriage is a three-strand cord consisting of God the Father, the husband, and the wife. This cord will maintain strength as long as God is the focus.

Courting offers many advantages that can save a couple from a long-suffering heartache and personal and spiritual loss. Dating, as opposed to courting, does not necessarily lead to marriage, and dating lacks biblical instruction and unconditional love because either mate can walk away from the relationship free of commitment. When a man and woman join together intimately, they give themselves away to each other in physical intimacy. A physical bond is made, and one's heart and body are given away. Does the other mate share that private bond, and are they willing to give unconditional love and to sacrifice one's needs for their companion? Or is it a superficial relationship wherein, once physical intimacy is achieved, it is followed by fleeting emotions by an irresponsible person merely looking only to please oneself?

The act of sex, when performed God's way, is physically satisfying and spiritually fulfilling to a marriage. When it is taken for granted and abused outside of marriage, a person receives pain, misery, and anguish. A man and woman who give their bodies away to each before a marriage commitment eventually suffer because they confused eros love, which is temporary, with agape love, which is sacrificial and responsible. We must be careful what we believe in our mind and who influences our mind. Patience, wisdom, and prayer will bring us our future mate. The best events in our life arrive when we least expect them. If we trust in God for our relationships, He will bless us with wonderful surprises. The worldly way of relationships is temporary, and men and women often treat each other like a piece of meat devoured and discarded because secular sex is carnal satisfaction. We are not pieces of meat offering ourselves to be devoured by a self-seeking person filling his or her insatiable carnal hunger. We are children of God, and He loves us and wants us to be loved with unconditional love.

The world has negatively influenced me, as I regarded marriage as a prison sentence rather than a companionship created by God. It wasn't until I studied the Bible and found the Lord's instruction for marriage. I also read a book on courting recently, and although the suggested steps appear archaic, virginal, and almost impossible to live out in an unscrupulous society, these guidelines work.

Why is God strict about saving sex for marriage to the point that sex His way appears flat and boring? We have been influenced to believe that lie. Sex is God's gift to us, but it is temporary and followed by lifelong unconditional companionship when we follow God's instruction. God made our bodies one way, His way. And He loves us and will never hurt us. "Everything is permissible, but not everything is beneficial. Everything is permissible, but not everything is constructive. Nobody should seek his own good, but the good of others" (1 Cor. 10:23–24).

Modern dating does not lead to nor promote a healthy marriage relationship. The term "hooking up" is another way of saying "I want to sleep with you a few nights, but I don't want to be responsible for you." Sex is a responsible commitment that leads to the creation of life. That's why it is called making love. The baby that is forming is conceived in the wife's body. The husband and wife join together sexually and spiritually, giving the baby life. This act is not selfish pleasure. Courting, unlike dating, can help a couple determine they have a harmonious and congruent companionship, putting on each other's needs first and saving sex for the marriage bed.

Courting may reveal severe incompatible differences in the relationship. This is a good thing for it is better to recognize those disagreeable issues in courtship and find, resolve, or end the relationship and remain amicable friends. In courtship, neither man nor woman gives their bodies away in physical intimacy. One can heal from lost emotional love, but you carry hurt from giving your body away because someone took intimacy away from you who did not take a vow of commitment to your body. That's in part what marriage is.

Only God can heal you from the pain of giving yourself away before marriage. A broken relationship is very sad; however, in a proper courtship where a man and woman save their purity, they can end the relationship without guilt or shame. You can still remain close friends and respect each other. From my own experience and other people, I have learned about the pain caused by giving yourself away before marriage. God designed sex for a husband and wife in marriage to enjoy. When our purity is taken outside of marriage, so is our innocence and trust. When the relationship fails, we are left broken, emotionally, mentally, and spiritually. This brokenness fuels anger toward the person who took our purity without commitment, and we pass on this animosity toward other mates in future unions of mistrust. A man or woman may give away his or her body to someone else in empty pursuit of self-pleasure. It becomes a sickness, and only God can cure this relationship disease if we turn to Him and live by His instruction.

Breaking a relationship with someone where sex is performed before marriage opens a man and woman to emotional wounds, along with physical and mental health problems, because they gave their body to someone who did not own their body by marital commitment. God's Word says that, in a marital relationship, a husband owns his wife's body. That is defined as no other man, but the husband sleeps with his wife. The wife owns her husband's body. No other woman but the wife sleeps with her husband. "The wife's body does not belong to her alone but also to her husband" (1 Cor. 7:4).

In the same way, the husband's body does not belong to him alone but also to his wife. The word "ownership" in this verse has a godly definition, unlike the earthly definition that is often held with vanity and selfish pride. Ownership in this case is defined as spouses promising and keeping their bodies between husband and wife in Christ. Confusion with Bible verses like the latter one is that we are grounded to earthly logic when it comes to word definitions that we don't search for the heavenly minded definition.

A wedding band is a symbol that a husband and wife

wear to publicly indicate the man and woman is each other's companion. Usually, the first item a single man and woman looks for is a wedding ring on the ring finger of that person of desirable interest. However if a husband and wife do not have a three-cord marriage, that is, having God as the center of their marriage, an affair can break that symbol. In many cases, a ring is just a challenge in our unscrupulous society. In an open relationship, there are no guidelines for caring and being responsible for each other. We are born of carnal nature, and there as we physically mature into adults, our bodies crave temporary pleasures. When we are filled, we go find another relationship with someone who is unaware that his or her heart will soon be broken. Heartache and personal emptiness will soon follow. Marriage shows an individual who he or she really is, and his or her spouse still loves him or her unconditionally. Only strong couples survive marital trials and crises that life throws at them, and that strength comes from the Lord and not within ourselves. "Jesus looked them and said 'With man this is impossible, but with God all things are possible'" (Matt. 19:26). No other relationship can go through fire without being burned. God's creation of marriage is the only fireproof relationship.

I want to end this chapter with an important prayer you can say together with your spouse. Maybe you never did anything like this before and you have nervousness or trepidation. Let me encourage you by this. Praying for your spouse is the best way you can defend and protect your spouse, marriage, and children. Remember there is an attack on God's marriage. Your marriage and your companionship may come under fire at some point in time. When it does, you will have developed a lifestyle practice of intimate prayer for your spouse. The enemy will retreat at the sight and sound of a husband and wife calling upon the name of the Lord to protect and save their marriage. If a husband and wife make this prayer time a lifestyle, just like physical fitness, with time and patience, they will both see evidence of the Lord working in their marriage.

When you have a few minutes together, follow this instruction. You may have to make time for this in a busy schedule, but think about the situations and climates that are ready to split a husband and wife apart into a world of anger bitterness, loneliness, and abandonment. That is not what God wants or intended for you. Don't let anything or anyone place a wedge in between you and your spouse! I want to walk you through this because I believe this is so important for lifelong companionship. Get together and find a quiet place in your home or car if you have to. I have listed some points below to pray about in your marriage:

- Do what is best for your spouse, and communicate.
- Respect the commitment of being husband and wife.
- Be still and just listen to your spouse. Don't be ready to fix anything or to have the last word.
- Forgive and forget faults and mistakes because both of you have them.
- Admit you are not perfect. Remember that practice makes improvement and perfection in people does not exist.
- Support each other in decisions that each of you make.
- Laugh, and don't forget to do this because we can all jest at our goofiness. Recognize that being goofy at proper times does not imply ignorance.
- Divide the strains of life when situations become rough.
- Support one another when matters are too hurried.
- Comfort each other in times when stress holds you down in worry.

- Be willing to adore your companion and friend whom God has blessed you in life with a joy and compassion.

I have included a prayer for both husband and wife below just to give you some help and ideas. Hold your wife's hand gently, and repeat this prayer:

> *Heavenly Father, thank you for my beautiful wife, friend, and companion you have blessed my life with. Lord, I pray she will have faithful eyes for me, patience, and understanding. Let me always express my love for her, and let me never forget that everything I do for her I also do for God because she is a child of God. Lord, help me to be the loving, patient, and trusting husband that my wife needs. Thank you heavenly Father for my wife. In Jesus' name. Amen.*

Hold your husband's hand gently, and say this prayer:

> *Heavenly Father, thank you for my handsome husband, friend, and companion you have blessed my life with. Lord, I pray he will have faithful eyes for me, patience, and understanding. Let me always express my love for him, and let me never forget that everything I do for him I also do for God because he is a child of God. Lord, help me to be the loving, patient, and trusting wife that my husband needs. Thank you, heavenly Father, for my husband. In Jesus' name. Amen.*

Marriage is a celebration between a husband and wife, companions whom God has placed together. May you always have biblical understanding to make your marriage work.

Chapter 4

The Church

I have had people tell me their reasons for not attending church. Some people have told me they believe there are churches that influence the faithful attend out of obligation and guilt. Others have said they believe in God but don't consider themselves religious. Other people have said the only thing the church wants is money. I have heard many people joke about the building falling down around them if they went. Some folks believe they are so terrible that God would not want them in His church.

They say, "If God knew what I have done, he wouldn't let me in His house."

It is very sad that lost, lonely, and hurting people are kept from church for these reasons and that they believe these lies. What is the purpose of the church? Jesus was the first to mention the church in Matthew 16:16–18. Simon Pete replied, "You are the Christ, the Son of the living God." And Jesus answered him,

> Blessed are you, Simon son of Jonah! For flesh and blood has not revealed this to you, but my Father who is in heaven. And I tell you, you are Peter, and on this

rock I will build my church, and the gates of hell shall not prevail against it.

Though many believe Jesus noted the meaning of Peter's name here as the rock, there was no supremacy given to him by Christ. Rather, Jesus was referring to Peter's declaration, "You are the Christ, the Son of the living God." This confession of faith is what the church is built upon, and just like Peter, everyone who confesses Jesus Christ as Lord is a part of the church. The church, therefore, is not a place. It is not the building, location, or denomination. We, God's people who are in Jesus Christ, are the church. The church is to be a place of fellowship where believers can be devoted to, honor, instruct, be kind and compassionate to, encourage, and, most importantly, love one another. The church is to be a place where believers can observe the Lord 's Supper, remembering Christ's death and shedding blood on our behalf.

The concept of "breaking bread" also carried the idea of having meals together. This is another example of the church promoting fellowship. The church is to be a place that promotes, teaches, and practices prayer. Philippians 4:6–7 encourages us, "Do not be anxious about anything, but in everything, by prayer and petition, with thanksgiving present your requests to God." Another commission given is proclaiming the gospel through Jesus Christ.

Jesus came to them and said "All authority in heaven and on earth has been given to me. Therefore go and make disciples of all nations, baptizing them in the name of the Father and of the Son and of the Holy Spirit, and teaching them to obey everything I have

commanded you. And surely I am with you always, to
the very end of the age" (Matt. 28:18–20).

In this verse, I believe all nations also refer to all cultures
of people who have never heard the gospel. Believers are called
to be faithful in sharing the gospel through word and deed
(personal actions). Believers are to be a "lighthouse" in the
community, shining their light onto other people and guiding
them toward Jesus Christ. Paul gives an excellent illustration
to the believers in Corinth what the church purpose is. The
church is God's people, a body of believers who are the hands,
mouth, and feet in this world, the body of Christ. We are to
be doing the things that Jesus Christ would do if He were here
physically on the earth. The body of believers is to be Christian,
Christlike, and Christ following.

A gathering of believers who bring the Holy Spirit within
themselves make the church. It is not the building. It is the
people who belong to God and proclaim Christ. A house of
worship can be an enormous building of great stature, or it
can be as simple and modest as the living room or basement
of a believer's home. Many believers open their homes to Bible
study. It is a very cozy setting to know that someone opened his
or her home to you. It makes you feel like a part of the family.
We bring God's spirit in us when we gather together. God is
love. "Dear friends, let us love one another, for love comes from
God. Everyone who loves has been born of God and knows
God. Whoever does not love does not know God, because God
is love" (1 John 4:7–8).

People gathered together in the Word grow in God's love,
and they are called the church body of believers. A person
invited by a friend to church may have trepidation about

attending. It takes courage to try something you've never done before. Imagine being invited to a place so personal like a place of worship, not knowing anyone except this friend you know or just met. What kind of atmosphere awaits that person willing to give this faith in God a try? Is that person going to be met at the door by a believer in Christ who is overjoyed to see him or her? Is this person going to experience the loving presence of Jesus Christ in this body of believers? Or is that church body going to blunder by giving that suffering, hurting child of God the indisputable body language that he or she is not welcome to this house of the Lord? Remember who the church body is, forgiven sinners who have chosen to serve the Lord. Hospitals are for physically sick and injured people. Churches are for spiritually sick and hurting people.

Believer, before that person walks through that door, is she or she going to be greeted by a Christian with the love of Christ and a genuine, warm smile? Or is he or she going to be judged by another sinner, which is who we all are? Remember, when you point your finger at someone, you have three fingers pointing right back at you!

The New Testament, as noted in latter part of this chapter, explains God's design for the church. Man's view of the church, however, is in dark contrast. Going to church is not about following rules, regulations, and obligations. On the contrary, it is about communion with God and giving Him glory and praise with a joyous heart. Our God is overflowing with His agape love, compassionate. He wants time with all of His children.

Most people connect church as a building where rules and regulations are to be followed; otherwise, we are betraying the church, and we are condemned to hell. When God commands us to do something He does it out of love for His creation. When man gives commands and rules it often leads to personal power rather than protection for humanity. God commands us to love one another and to forgive one another. In religion, we do good works for those we feel deserve it and for whom we like. Those we don't like, we don't go out of our way for. Religion does not require that we love or forgive all people. But God is very honest in His Word and reveals what he expects from us. Having religion and doing things that make us look good is very easy, but faith and doing something for somebody we don't like is impossible unless we see that person as a child of God.

God dwells within those who call upon His presence. I have read articles in magazine and news articles describing buildings from old movie houses to vacant factories renovated into churches. The idea of church is about people who gather in the building and God who is dwelling in the people. Believers gathering in an open, grassy field welcoming the presence of the Lord with songs of praise and reading the Word are church.

What does worship mean? It is a service showing reverence for the Lord, an intense love and admiration. Worship music is deepened when you grow stronger by studying the Word of God. Worship is allowing yourself to be filled with the joy-filled music and singing songs of praise and glory to our God and King. This time of spiritual harmony will give you a peace in your heart and your mind as you welcome it. Worship is not an obligation. God does not force anyone to worship Him. This is a personal choice. That's why he created us. He gave us a free will. To most unbelieving people, this is very weird behavior, but then having a forgiving and loving nature probably seems strange as well.

Most Christ-centered churches begin service with music and praise. I heard this music for the first time in the Pentecostal church I attended. I also started listening to praise and worship music on my Christian radio station. At first, it was strange to me because I was not accustomed to listening to music that praised God. It wasn't the same old-time organ music that you hear on old television shows or movies. I grew up listening to rock and roll, both classic and modern rock and especially heavy metal when working out while lifting weights. (Although now I favor contemporary Christian rock as my genre, the Newsboys "God's Not Dead" is an excellent workout song.) I realized most of the rock songs that I listened to before Christ are dedicated to good times, self-pleasures, and a physical love relationship that no one seems able to keep or want for long. I've heard that old adage, "Rock and roll is the devil's tongue," and I would laugh when I heard it years back. After reading verses that refer to entertaining dark spirits, Leviticus 19:26 says, "Do not practice divination or sorcery." I was surprised how many songs had extremely dark lyrics that glorified a wasted and abused life. I also realized that, while the sounds of heavy metal rock were cool, I wasn't aware of the dark, carnal lyrics that the hypnotic modulation of drums and steel guitars deafened. I researched certain songs I listened to in those days and discovered the lyrics I was rocking to in an intoxicated state were about sex performed outside of marriage. These lyrics were about sex acts that left a person empty and abandoned. Are we conscious that we are capable of treating each other like a full bag of garbage? Once we have exhausted our pleasures, we throw them away. But music that praises the Lord our God does not croon of self-pleasures or glorifying man. On the contrary, the music composition describes God's love for us in the sacrifice of His Son for our transgressions and the promise of a new resurrected life through Christ. If God was that furious with us and thought we were not worth saving, some people believe he would have disowned us right in the beginning. But He loves us because we are His creation despite our sin nature. He does love us, or He would not have allowed His Son Jesus to endure the suffering and agony He went through. Jesus Christ in the Bible is proof of God's love for us. He gave us the ability to make our own decisions when He started with Adam and Eve. He could have ended with them, but He did not. He is the God of possibilities, and He blesses us with opportunities. That's what these worship songs are about. Everything God has done for us is told in these songs of praise.

He is not dead. Our God is alive, and His spirit dwells in all who believe in Him and His Son. Before I received Christ, I never heard a rock song that praised the God of heaven until I listened to Christian rock. Some bands can really rock in praise music.

Music is a time to allow yourself to be filled with God's presence. Our music today has many genres. Although there are colorful and rhythmic melodies, they pale in comparison to music composed for the glory of God. Praise and worship music moves a person's soul with inspiration and regeneration. Most modern music artists sing or write songs that glorify the satisfaction of one's own self. Seldom do modern music artists sing or compose songs of praise to our God and King, although there are a few exceptions in a few genres. The praise music that we sing is based on what God has done for this earth and mankind. God breathed life onto our planet. He led oppressed and weary people to lands that were bountiful in a harvest that could support and nourish life in us. He blessed people from all walks of life to a new land full of milk and honey and wealth and prosperity. We call this land our great home, America. Yet for everyone who has been blessed, rarely does God receive the praise. It is God with whom we are blessed with our talents and skills.

Most people, it seems, assume that God is an angry god who is just waiting us to do something wrong so He can send us to hell. God is not waiting for us to mess up so He can cast curses upon us. If we read the Bible, we are told that God wants to bless our lives and fill us with joy. The Bible tells us that God is love. He doesn't need to be refilled or reenergized. Love flows endlessly from the God of heaven. I wonder if God cries when His children deny any gift they have to the one who gave us life in the womb. When I listen to these worship songs, I am so grateful that my eyes were spiritually opened and my heart was filled with His love. The worship music opens you to the word of God.

Denomination is defined as a particular religious body. There are many denominations, but the term "born again" is what Jesus explained to Nicodemus the Pharisee, but Nicodemus could not understand. "In reply Jesus declared 'I tell you the truth, no one can see the kingdom of God unless he is born-again'" (John 3:3). Perhaps this Pharisee was thinking of earthly terms that he could not see life in heavenly understanding. Nicodemus did not understand this claim from the Son of God, and even today, people cannot comprehend this born-again faith.

Adam and Eve were the first human creations who opened the door to sin, so basically we have all inherited their sin. When we are born, we are born of the flesh and prone to sin. It is not until we arrive at a point in our life when we are capable of knowing right from wrong that we can make a decision of faith to live for Christ. A child raised in faith and biblical instruction may come to receive salvation at an early age. However, an individual may not be ready to receive Christ until later in his or her life. We come to a point in our life when we can decide on our own. Receiving faith in Christ is not made by coercion or force. It is a personal decision that a person makes at an accountable age. Influences and a child's upbringing can be beneficial to receiving faith or a hindrance in one receiving eternal salvation.

So what is it like to experience one of these born-again services? It really depends on the style of church having the service. I have witnessed both reserved services where there is worship music and quite a few spirit-filled believers raising their hands in praise to the music. I have also beheld services that include a raise of hands, shouts of "Hallelujah" and "Praise the Lord," and some anointed believers speaking a prophetic word and others speaking in tongues.

What in the world is speaking in tongues? Pastor Lou explained this to me. "When you open your heart to the Lord, He speaks through you, and you start speaking words that may sound like complete gibberish, but only God know exactly what you are saying."

Pastor Lou added one more fascinating detail. "The enemy of our faith gets nervous when we speak in tongues because he does understand what we are saying only God does."

My pastors throughout my walk of faith have been given such a gift of spiritual insight that religion could never give me. To most people who are not open to this personal and spiritual freedom, as a result of this born-again experience, these people appear to be radical religious nutcases. I came to the same verdict before I received my faith, but I also had a personal emptiness, and I would not give up until I found the truth. Even before I entered that church where Pastor Lou asked if I received Christ as my Savior, I was praying unceasingly to know and better understand God. What causes this strange behavior that believers sing and dance, shout glory to the Lord, and speak in tongues? Many people view this as very crazy behavior. As opposed to what? Drinking, drugging, and uncontrolled sexual behavior? Beating other human beings in a selfish, violent rampage? I look at it this way. If my mouth is too busy glorifying God and proclaiming the gospel, I don't have time or desire to mock, gossip, or discourage anyone in my life. I remember in my childhood hearing that born agains are a religious sect. However, religion is based on laws that God knew we would never keep. Just look at the Ten Commandments. Knowing that, in God's character, He has plans for our redemption should bring a person into a joyous attitude. As strange and abnormal as this behavior appears to be, I now understand why believers act this way in church.

Before I received Christ as my personal Savior, I had doubt, fear, and unanswered questions about life. Is there really a purpose in life? When I open the Bible, I look up a particular verse for that situation that is disturbing me. By reading the Word and accepting it, my fears and doubts have been removed, and my questions have been answered (in God's timing, not mine). We all have a purpose in life, as I discovered in the Bible. We were not created to live mundane lives just paying taxes and then dying. An abundant and fruitful life is awaiting us in God's plan, but we have to ask for it, just as we were taught as children to ask. After all, God is our heavenly Father. All of this is why believers get excited in music worship. The chains of the pain of this sinful earthly life have been broken. Believers don't have to do good works and hope they are still good enough to get to heaven. We have received Christ, the payment for our sins, so we can know we are going to heaven based on what Jesus did for us. We don't have to go through life with doubts of our eternity or our future. We act this way because of the joy we receive through Christ, and the music we hear speaks to us because the harmonious sound is alive. Faith is about being alive and living in joy despite pain. The Bible describes the same joyful dancing and singing in heaven. Well, if all of heaven is rejoicing with our God and King, why not prepare for the celebration here on the earth now?

Religion on the contrary is idle and does not reach out to lost and hurting people. Religion is just man's way to get to heaven by himself without a savior. Sacrificial love defeats hate and unforgiveness, which is sin. The only way to enter heaven is through Jesus—the doorway to God the Father. If you don't have Jesus, then you don't have God. Faith is believing what we cannot see. So when I am among my fellow believers expressing their gratitude and joy in this manner, I understand this freedom that comes from the Lord. Sunday morning is not a funeral service. It is not a day of guilt or obligation either. Sunday is a celebration. Actually, it is a special day to get together with other believers. Every day in Christ is a celebration. God made rules such as the Ten Commandments, which we cannot keep. In the New Testament, Jesus gave us God's instructions how to live a healthy and joyous life despite our fallen, sinful nature. He became the final sacrifice, and in Him, we have life here on this earth while we wait for God to call us home for eternity. Religion cannot give us life here on this earth in our flesh, and religion cannot guarantee our passage to heaven. Only a relationship with Jesus Christ can give us life. Gathering with other believers and studying the Word of God deepens our understanding. Listening to personal testimonies of believers who were transformed from an empty self-condition to a new fulfilling life creation inspires hope to a hopeless person.

I performed an online research for the word "enthusiasm" and discovered a theological find. The word comes from the Greek form *enthousiasmos*, from *enthousiazein* "to be inspired," from *entheos* "inspired," and from en- + *theos* "God." So enthusiasm comes from God. The Bible speaks to us that heaven is a real, tangible place filled with music and the sweet fragrance of the Father Son and Holy Spirit. All of heaven is in triumphant chorus to God and His Son, our risen Savior.

Our earthly time in praise and singing is just a rehearsal session to get warmed up for our jubilant family reunion with our heavenly Father. If we open our hearts and receive Christ as our Savior and then allow Him to change us from the inside, He will work through us. This will also allow His spirit to move in us. A loving God created us. We were also given the ability to make choices. God is often blamed for all the bad events that happen in life. Perhaps a person's bad decision when shunning God's will for our life causes some bad events. Maybe the bad things that happen in our society are the examples of how humans act when they don't live by God's instruction. God does not cause bad.

How can sacrificial love cause bad? Once again, it all started in the garden. God told Adam and Eve not to eat that certain fruit. The serpent told them, if they ate the fruit, they could be equal to God in knowledge. But God has no equal. They were already like God made in His image. So the serpent lied, and they bought it. Generations have continued to do what these two started in the garden, to rebel and live life our own way and to be God's equal in knowledge. Let God be God. He knows what He's doing, and let us be servants.

When I first observed this praise and worship, dancing in the aisle, and talking in tongues, it was very strange behavior to me. But as bizarre as it appeared to me, I noticed that the people around me who had this joy did not look imprisoned. What I mean is they had troubles. Their lives were not peachy. But they did not allow these circumstances to control them; nor did they live a dead life. No, these people I witnessed up-front and personal were alive with joy, not zombies walking around in misery and pain. I was always worried what people in my life would think about me if they saw me doing in church what my fellow believers were doing.

I believe many of us worry about what others will think when we do something out of the ordinary. When we do this, we are allowing other people to control us. Besides, what's wrong with doing something that leads to enthusiasm and ambition versus mundane bland, especially when our freedom comes from God? We try to please people we can never please. Now I'm not saying we should not serve people who are disagreeable and unpleasant. The problem is that we tend to please people with expectation that we will turn that person around and perhaps receive self-glory for it. We should love others and serve them for the glory of God, not out of expectation or reciprocation.

I know I have placed my faith and trust in people and, most often, have been left disappointed. We pass our good works around and expect our deeds to be returned to us. Thoughts of "kickback" and "what's in it for me" often follow a motive for doing something. We live by expectation, and because perfection does not exist in human beings, we are often disappointed in other people. We should not expect anything in return for what we do, but we should receive all blessings that God has stored up for us. What other people think of us often control us. And oftentimes, we walk softly, not wanting to offend anyone. What about offending God who made heaven and earth, who guided persecuted people to a new land where they could give glory to the God of heaven? Our Creator created man and then woman so man would not be alone but have a life companion. What about offending our heavenly Father who loves us and gave us His own Son so we could live in eternity when our physical bodies turn to dust? We were created to please and worship God our Father, but because of Adam and Eve, we also made wrong choices and chose to worship ourselves. Our flesh controls us.

Another destination is waiting for us to make a choice. There is no joy and celebration there, and Christ does not reside there. The Bible speaks of the one who waits for those who deny Christ the risen Savior. He is the father of all lies. He waits for those who deny Jesus Christ despite the truths given to them on earth. Here in the land of abandon separated from God, there is no party, dancing, and good times with good friends, as many worldly songs claim in their lyrics. The Bible makes no mistakes about it. Why does this place even exist, and why did God make such a place? Heaven's fallen angel made the wrong choice when he wanted to take over heaven in selfish gain. Hell, the lake of fire, as the Bible describes, is where those who do not love God are sent. God does not send anyone there. Where we go for eternity is our choice based on how we choose to live on earth. If we don't forgive and love like God does and give that love and forgiveness toward others, how can we live with God? We love and forgive other people; or we choose not to.

If we choose not to forgive and love others, there is only one place to dwell. How can we live eternally with God if we don't love God? God and His only begotten Son sit on their throne in heaven, waiting to receive those who have chosen the Father's Son as their personal Savior and His grace. We bow down to God in the presence of His love, not in fearful terror of a forceful god. We bow by our own choice because He has shown His love for us in the life, death, and resurrection of his Son Jesus Christ, our Lord and Savior.

I believe God cries when His children make a bad decision of their own free will. Again, our will to live against God casts us into eternal damnation. It is our choice, not God's. A person who does not forgive or love people and God, as well as denies His deity, cannot enter heaven. To be born again is to be born in Christ, to be made a new creation, a spiritual birth. If a person's logic is grounded on earthly thinking, heaven-bound thinking will not make sense.

It used to concern me what other people thought of me. But when I received Christ as my Savior and read the Bible on my own, I became more concerned about what God thinks of me. The Bible tells me that God loves me and He's crazy about me. God is jealous for me. I did not think I could be that close to God, but the Bible tells me I can. Before I read the Bible, I never heard these words before. What other people think of me does not matter now that the true word of God has been made known to me. Whatever I do here on earth I will do in heaven because I have a relationship and a lifestyle with my God. And this joyful behavior will be welcomed with open arms in heaven!

Sadly, this freedom to exercise our faith may be taken away here in America as our nation continues to demand that God be taken out of America completely. Evidence of God slowly removing His protective hand from America is being revealed in the animal kingdom among other areas. God controls the animal kingdom, and even wild beasts are under His control. But in recent years, many animals are showing signs that they are not afraid of human beings. God is withdrawing His protection because our nation has asked Him to leave by removing the Bible, prayer, and the Ten Commandments and ignoring His biblical instruction. One should tremble at the thought of a godless America and a nation of ungodly citizens.

When I read the Word of God and then briefly look at the news headlines of the day, it is amazing that, while this is news to us, these events are already foretold in the Bible as they unfold today. The Bible describes us like sheep, and sheep have no direction unless they have a shepherd to guide them. God is talking to us through His Word and other believers. He is reaching out in His love, and we are given His mercy, but eventually enough will be enough. If America does not want God and all His abundant blessings, He will honor America's request and walk away, and we will lose His blessing and protection. Remember, we have been attacked, but we have never been plundered. We are still free America so far. It is not too late to turn our country back to God. We can turn the sadness, loss, and gloom that we face as a nation into hope and joy if we turn in the direction of the one who can give us His bright and glorious light.

The Word of God tells us that our problem is sin, along with what the solution is, believing that God's only Son Jesus Christ died on the cross for our sins and God resurrected Him from the dead. Now He is seated on the right side of our heavenly Father. I learned this through Bible studies and reading the

Bible in my own time. God does not barge in our life and bark orders at us. When we realize that our way is not working in our lives and we allow the Holy Spirit to reside in us, the Lord takes away the spiritual dead weight that is keeping us from receiving joy and holding us in physical, mental, and spiritual bondage. When we receive the Lord in our heart, He fills us with a joy that cannot be contained or suppressed. His redemption unshackles us, and we are no longer bound in chains of anger, depression, anxiety, self-centeredness, emptiness, and low self-worth. When we hear worship music, we hear freedom, and the presence of the Lord fills us. We don't need a building to hear music. We don't even need devices because we make our own joyful sound to our God and King. We want to dance and shout praises to the Lord. We are not ashamed to express joy because we are saved through Jesus Christ! When a person truly receives Christ in his or her heart, He will show in his or her actions. When we allow Christ to takes residence in us, revenge, anxiety, or fear of our future have no room to dwell. Anger is a normal human response; however, it is dangerous when we let this emotion control us, for out of it we seek revenge. For the Lord to take residence in our hearts, we have to allow Christ to "clean" our hearts so He can move in. He brings everything that He embodies into us. A believer is no longer a prisoner of worry, bitterness, unforgiveness, and doom of the future. We do not deny the events that are unfolding or the states of mind these events bring to us. Actually by reading the Bible, we already know of these events, along with why they are happening. We have a choice, and we can give our worries and fears to our God, who is in control. (There is a great song titled "God Is in Control.") We were made to love and adore Him. We have been given a free will to choose how we want to live and make our own decisions. We perform duties and serve other people out of love, appreciation, and gratitude for what God did for us. We serve others to glorify God, not ourselves. Others choose not to give God any reverence or recognition. Perhaps the reason is because of influences around us. We are not encouraged to love God but to love and worship ourselves and material objects.

The Bible refers to the church as the body of Christ's disciples gathering for fellowship, and that is the definition of church. Sadly, there are Christians who are filled with Christ, and then they stop the glass in the middle. They don't allow themselves to be filled to overflowing from their cup of joy. They don't allow Christ to finish "cleaning up" their heart, and they end up moving back old "roommates" or past baggage into their heart. It is important that a believer, especially one who is new in his or her faith, focus on biblical teaching and study with other believers. Christianity is a faith of action. After all, Jesus is our leader, and while He was on earth, He initiated actions of love, healing, and praying that we believers should be continuing until He calls us for our homecoming. Jesus instructed His apostles on the living Word of God, and His Word lives today as He will be there when we who believe we are His apostles and two or more gather in His presence anywhere. Convene with people who call upon the presence of God in Jesus' name in their home study. Prayerfully consider a church where believers call upon the presence of God and they proclaim the message of salvation and biblical instruction through Jesus Christ. Don't look for a perfect church or perfect people because perfection does not exist in human beings. Instead, look for an imperfect body of believers worshipping God our Father and His Son, Jesus Christ.

There are many lies about God. One of them is that He is an angry god who waits with His judgment for those who do wrong so he can send them to hell as though He has a sadistic nature. God is not angry at His children. On the contrary, He is concerned about us. He is love. While it is true He hates ungodly actions, He does not hate His creations, us His children. Hatred is an emotion man has toward fellow human beings, and it is by choice. Hatred is often taught and handed down from generation upon generation. People hate for many reasons. They choose to have hardened, unforgiving hearts, spiritually speaking. God loves all of His children. He does not want His children to be harmed. The unwise and ungodly choices grieve God. Yes, God grieves at the result of our unwise choices that hurt us.

Take, for example, a child who is taught about fire safety and told not to play with matches. By our own curiosity, elements such as fire fascinate us. We get too close, and in our rebellion against authority, we are burned because we chose not to listen to the consequences of misusing fire. Many "fires" (selfish desires) in life will burn us if we get too close. If we continue to ignore God's warnings before us, these "fires" or bad choices will consume us. God knows how we are, and oftentimes, it takes a hurt to get our attention of impending danger, and we may still ignore His warning. Our stubbornness increases our rebellion. We blame God for our pain and hurt.

In truth, God is not the one hurting us. We are hurting ourselves by not listening to our loving and living God. Suppose God appeared to us in person and spoke in an audible voice. Would we really hear and see Him? Would we truly listen to what He had to say with understanding? Or would we keep our hearts and eyes closed to the message of God and pass Him off as a lunatic?

As long as we think we can go through this life without God, the things that hurt us will continue to do so. When we start listening to God and stop doing the things that hurt us, only then will we be transformed. God provides the wisdom and knowledge we need. Will we accept it or turn away and continue with our own life plan? Or will we trust God with the fulfilling life plan that He has written for our lives? There are people who either don't believe or refuse to believe in the written Word and living evidence of God. They will reject godly wisdom, but for those who choose to believe, love, joy, and forgiveness will fill their lives. Those who choose to believe will have abundant life and the promise of eternal life through Jesus Christ. God wants us to gather with other believers and to continue that fellowship even after Sunday service is over to maintain accountability and to encourage our walk of faith. The time we spend with God is not a ninety-minute feel-good meeting.

I recall attending Sunday service with my family and pretending to listen to the message. I was relieved when the sermon was over. I did my Sunday obligation, and now I could go my way, act like a jerk to everyone, and do whatever I wished to do. Then I could go back to the next Sunday service and start the good churchgoing person façade all over again.

I use the word *believer* numerous times and for good reason. Many Christians live this good churchgoing life, but they are not transformed. Those who believe live what they learn from the Bible. It is a practiced lifestyle of faith in action, not preached. Religion is often known as living by laws and still being a jerk to other people. Faith is love and transforms a person to love others. Even a Christian can have a spiritual heart problem.

Maybe you don't attend church because the congregants there treated you like you don't belong. God created the church as a body of believers who respect one another and create an atmosphere of acceptance as children of God. If you are not experiencing that, maybe you need to be with a body of believers who do walk in this way.

Let me share something humorous and profound with you. An elderly African American gentleman has been praying to God that this church the man wished to attend would let him in to worship and praise God. But the people of that church refused and kept telling him he was not welcome.

A long period of time has passed, and the man prays unceasingly with sorrow, "Lord, I want to worship you, but they won't let me in."

Then one day, the Lord answers this weeping man who is deep in prayer. He hears the voice of the Almighty in his heart. "My son, I am sad with you. I have been trying for many years to get in this house, but they won't let me in either."

Although I heard this told as joke, sadly, in some real situations, it is very true. So whose house it is anyway, God's or man's? Since the time I have become a believer, I have noticed a growing trend in born-again churches, and that is the zeal to become a mega church. Many churches are aiming at bigger congregations. While this is a tenacious goal to set forth, we must be careful that no believers are left behind in this quest for great numbers of the faithful. It is of the utmost priority that every faithful servant be well studied in Scripture and focused on bringing lost souls to Christ. It is equally important that believers are active in community outreaches. Jesus tells the parable of the lost sheep.

Luke 15:4-7 "Suppose one of you has a hundred sheep and loses one of them. Does he not leave the ninety-nine in the open country and go after the lost sheep until he finds it? And when he finds it, he joyfully puts it on his shoulders and goes home. Then he calls his friends and neighbors together and says, 'Rejoice with me; I have found my lost sheep. I tell you that in the same way there will be more rejoicing in heaven over one sinner who repents than over ninety-nine righteous persons who do not repent."

Aspiring to have a spacious building to praise and worship God should not be clouded with an architectural idea that will be glorified instead of our Lord. The purpose of our mission is to establish room to grow and populate with saved souls and marriages, not to enter *Popular Churches and Gardens* magazine. We must not diverted from the purpose of God's plan for the church, to teach the gospel of the Lord Jesus Christ and reach a lost and dying world. So believer in Christ, when you enter the Lord's house, bring the love of Christ that dwells within you.

The church I attend has a growing number of faithful believers. Our music worship team is a humble group of people who have a zeal for the Lord. There are people from various cultural backgrounds and occupations. There is no set dress code, so the way you are dressed is not an issue. Christ is the focus of our church. When I started attending this chapel four years ago, I sensed a strong presence of the Lord. I wanted to give a money offering so this church could reach others with the gospel, but I noticed no baskets were being passed around. I did notice these small boxes hanging on the wall by the entrances to the sanctuary. On my second visit, I read the church bulletin and realized the wooden boxes attached to the walls were collection boxes. This amazed me—no one hovering over you waiting for you to drop money into a basket. No pressure! You give discreetly what you can afford to the kingdom of God, and it is between you and God.

> Remember this; Whoever sows sparingly will also reap sparingly, and whoever sows generously will also reap generously. Each man should give what he has decided in his own heart to give, not reluctantly or under compulsion, for God loves a cheerful giver (2 Cor. 9:6–7).

There is no wrong or right way to collect the offering; however, it is nice to know that the collection is not the focus of your visit to church. God's love for us is.

I have heard often the phrase, "That person has more money than God." We were born naked, and anything we think we own belongs to God. One day material possessions will be destroyed because God has a better plan for us in heaven that will eternally fulfill us. Somewhere I heard this bit of insight. The only man-made thing in heaven that we will see is the nail wounds in Jesus' hands and feet when he was hung on our cross. Jesus took the hit for all of us.

I believe God uses the resource of money to see where our hearts are, along with to see how we use it and if we are wise stewards of our money. Do we use our monetary blessings to bless others? Or do we use our money to get power and control of which we cannot, in our own self, maintain in unity.

Another form of church outreach is missions. I think of missions as a traveling church, a body of believers in Christ who go to foreign lands where the message of salvation has never been heard and where the Bible has never been read or available. First, these believers take action and serve the daily needs of people and, in doing so, show the love of Christ in their actions. Then the message is offered in love, not forcefully thrust upon that person or people. Many Americans receive God's calling to serve in other nations. I have met some people in missions who describe accounts in foreign lands where people who dare to assemble a Bible study are incarcerated or killed for their belief in Christ. They also report that some new believers have hidden in underground cellars for personal safety in order to study the Bible as a group and worship the Lord. Imagine a country where its people are forbidden to assemble and pray for hope and peace in the name of the Lord. Our history tells us that the pilgrims came to America to escape religious persecution and practice their faith in freedom. Today, it is evident that America is going in the opposite direction and denying freedom of faith that made our land so great and prosperous.

The people who serve missions also describe living conditions in countries much less fortunate than America—sleeping on dirt floors, drinking muddy water, and having no technological conveniences. It's just a poor and primitive way of living. These conditions are far from the privileges God blesses America with. These people are open to God's Word when our American missionaries bring our blessed bounty to them. America is a land where our ancestors risked a potentially perilous voyage from a land of persecution for one's faith to a land where a family can practice their faith in freedom to the one true God in whom real freedom and liberty is established.

Hurting people are out there. As the Scripture says in Luke 10:2 "The harvest is plentiful, but the workers are few. Ask the Lord of the harvest, therefore, to send out workers into his harvest field." Now more than ever, America, one nation under God, needs believers, fellow human beings who are willing to go out of their way to help the helpless. If Jesus were to come to earth right now and survey the body of believers whom He commissioned through His Word to help heal and pray for those who don't know the Savior of the world, how many would He find? Every human being should experience the love and healing of Jesus Christ and God the Father when they enter that holy gathering place called the body of Christ. A Christ-centered church teaches the Bible and salvation, and it encourages and inspires the love of God. People dwell on so much gloom that a person is mired in discouragement and hopelessness. There are many lies and many ways to be deceived that it can cause a person to live a skeptical and joyless life of misery. Believers not grounded in the Word of God can be misled down that path of destruction. The Bible gives a believer guidance and hope, and it exposes those lies and their source. It is a relief to know that God is in control. And if he is for us, who can be against us? Attending Sunday church service is a "shower" for our soul to wash the dirt and filth that we receive when walking in the world.

Why go to church more than once a week? Well, our bodies need a shower or bath every night. Our souls are no different in the filth that covers us. This time in the Lord fills us with love and hope in a hopeless and loveless world. We need to be reenergized in love, encouragement, inspiration, and hope. We can never get enough of God. He gives us peace where mankind brings fear. There is an acronym for FEAR—False Evidence Appearing Real.

I began my walk twelve years ago, I have had trials and crises in my life, and I have made some very poor decisions as a believer because I thought I achieved perfection through faith. Faith is not perfection. It is transformation and improvement. Perfection is saved for heaven. Even though I am born again, I have still hurt some people and even betrayed a few close friends. But in His Word, Jesus never promised that I would not have problems in this new life He gave me. I believe in those times when I let people down, I thought I'd be flawless in my faith. He wanted to show me that I'm not going to be perfect, and I also believe He was and continues to work on my pride problem. Sometimes we believers, Christians, have this false thinking that we are untouchable because our faith will make us perfect. That's when conceit settles in us. We chose Christ because we do have faults and failures; however, we shouldn't allow our fallen nature to control us. We will always have that faulty nature with us until we are called home. If Jesus took it away, we would not see the need to follow Him from this temporary earthly life to our eternal home in heaven, where all believers in Christ will live in eternal light and love. Amen to that! God bless you, and God bless the church.

Chapter 5

The Bible

I am not writing this chapter as a biblical expert. I am writing this as a guide to the truths revealed and the discoveries of personal accounts that have been made clear to me through study. I am a student in continuous pursuit of biblical instruction. Many people ask, "How can we know the Bible is true after all? Man has rewritten it, and there are numerous editions."

The arguments and rebuttals on this subject are endless. I have been researching the Bible even deeper while I write this book to make sure what I quote is from the Word of God and not my own words. I have given my thoughts and opinions in this book, but I have written the verses exactly as I see them in the Bible. Let's say someone asks me to revise a paper for him or her that he or she has written about me and asks me not to change the way he or she describes me. In that person's truthful point of view, he or she describes me as a slanderous, lying, cheating, self-seeking person with evil thoughts. First of all, I would tell that person what he or she could do with that paper. Before I read the Bible, I had this image of myself being a good person. Yes, I have made mistakes, but my good works will cover me, or so that's what I believed. The Word of God has revealed what kind of person I really am, the kind of person we all are because of our fallen nature. I would never rewrite a book that compares me to an animal that lacks common sense and wit, as in a sheep. The Bible insults our selfish pride, but God's loves His creation. Only in Christ can we accomplish great victories. In Mark 10:22, Jesus said, "With man this is impossible, but not with God; All things are possible with God."

While reading some of the Scripture for the first time, I came across a verse that was unsettling to me. This verse describes us being as a filthy rag. "All of us have become like one who is unclean, and all our righteous acts are like filthy rags; we shrivel up like a leaf, and the wind sweeps us away" (Isa. 64:6). So the Bible is truthful about our condition, which is disturbing to some who will read it. The Bible continues to say that none of our good works will cover or clean the filth of our sin. "For the wages of sin is death, but the gift of God is eternal life in Jesus Christ our Lord" (Rom. 6:23).

The Bible does not hide anything. The Word exposes the bad news and declares the good. God always has a solution to our problems. Parts of the Bible are very insulting to human beings. 1 Peter 2:25 may sound very debasing to us. Farmers and sheep owners say this about sheep; they have to be guarded because, if one falls off a cliff, each one of the herd will follow. I gave this some serious thought when I read it for the first time. We are like sheep in that any false word or evidence can convince us to walk away from God. I know I have had a difficult time admitting when I'm wrong, and that is a pride problem. Also, maybe we don't admit we are wrong because it may imply we are clumsy and incompetent. A wise man admits his mistakes and grows stronger in solutions; a foolish man, however, falls off his pedestal in pride. Our pride and arrogant natures hinder us from loving people in sacrificing our time and labor for someone we don't know or whom we hold animosity. God cannot show His love through arrogant and prideful people. That is one reason a new believer may experience trouble.

A personal trial is God's way of turning our vain and haughty nature into a Christlike nature. This process is very painful to one's ego. I have experienced this, but it happened for my own good. Otherwise, I would not be open to hear the cry of our hurting humanity.

Every day, I learn about God's nature when I study the Word reverently. The Bible is God's truth that love is alive. It's not just some old, dusty, mythical novel. The Word is full of human action, drama, sacrifice, and comedy. Before I commenced reading these living accounts of our human race, the men and women in these recorded events in the Bible sounded like folklore when I heard it as a child in church.

When I was a young boy, my mother recounted the Bible stories handed down to her. Among the bedtime Bible stories that she read to me was Noah's Ark. From the story, Noah was a great man of God. God commanded him to build the ark, for God was going to destroy the earth because no one except Noah and his family obeyed God and lived a life pleasing to Him. Everyone around Noah mocked him, for there was no logical reason for the ark because the region was dry and arid with not even a rain cloud in sight. But Noah obeyed God's command, and he and his family, along with the birds and animals, were spared. That's the gist of Noah's life from this story.

Another Bible hero was Moses. According to the story (and I'm paraphrasing), he parted the Red Sea and led his people out of slavery from Egypt. The rest of the story I received when

I saw the movie; however, I still had questions since I was only a young child.

The stories my mother told my from the New Testament came with more spiritual insight. When I was a teenager, I came close to a Christ-centered home Bible study. Matter of fact, my friend's brother was welcomed to this study. He shared the story of Jacob's ladder with us other neighbor kids. Of course, this Bible-reading stuff sounded crazy, and I was apprehensive, if I attended this study, the local kids would tease me like they were teasing my friend's brother. I received enough mocking and teasing in my teenage years. I wasn't about to follow these weird, Bible-reading Holy Rollers.

When I accepted Christ as my personal Savior in January 2001, Pastor Lou encouraged me to read the Bible, and he gave me specific men of the Bible to study. He learned from our conversations that I had a superficial knowledge of the apostles and he recommended that if I studied them in depth I would realize they were ordinary fallible men just like me. The most amazing description was John the Baptist a rugged man who ate locust and honey. From my childhood I pictured men of the bible like John the Baptist as appearing clean cut and wearing fine robes because they were not described as ordinary men. He also told me that God wants to use me for His glory. That stunned me. How could God use me? I'm not a great man like those men I heard about in the Bible. From the stories I understood, these men were perfect and did no wrong. My first few years as a new believer, I read the New Testament, and through the Easter productions that I participated in, I was able to study the characters of those disciples. They were not the stained glass images of perfection I believed they were. The apostles were ordinary men who followed their call from the Lord. In modern slang, they could be called knuckleheads. Peter denied Jesus. Matthew was a tax collector, and society did not like him well. Judas was out for money and sold out the Savior. I read about the garden of Gethsemane account where Jesus requests they stay awake. But they end up falling asleep instead of remaining steadfast prayer warriors. These tough guys, some fisherman, were a motley crew for Jesus Christ, but as messed up and argumentative as they were, the Lord still used them to spread the gospel.

Four years ago, I made an ambitious attempt to read the Bible all the way though in one year. In that year, I only made it to 1 Chronicles, but I did manage to get some very important facts about some of the Old Testament men. I read about Noah and the ark, but for the first time, an important factor was revealed about this so-called perfect man.

> Noah, a man of the soil, proceeded to plant a vineyard. When he drank some of its wine, he became drunk and lay uncovered inside his tent. Ham, the father of Canaan, saw his fathers nakedness and told his two brothers outside. But Shem and Japheth took a garment and laid it across their shoulders; then they walked in backward and covered their fathers nakedness. Their faces were turned the other way so that they would not see their fathers nakedness (Gen. 9:20–23).

Noah's two sons found him drunk and naked. There goes the perfect man of the Bible theory. When I read this, I praised God for revealing this truth. I remember my drinking days, and now I can imagine how embarrassing I must have been, although I always kept my clothes on. I have been sober since

December 23, 2001. By the grace of God, my daughter will never have to endure the embarrassment of an intoxicated father. So Noah wasn't a perfect man, but God used him anyway because he had a heart for God. More can be learned about Noah in Genesis 5. Maybe God can use me after all.

I discovered facts about another man in the Bible, Moses. What I did know was that he was a leader of his people. He parted the Red Sea, and he witnessed the burning bush that was not being consumed in flames. These things were told to me in church, but it wasn't until I read the Bible with my own eyes that Moses' imperfections were revealed to me. He intervened in the beating of a salve and killed a man. He was known for his temper, and he had a speech impediment. He reacted in situations in his own self rather than responding in God's time. Despite Moses' fallible human qualities, he had a heart for God, and he was available to serve God. More can be learned about Moses in the book of Exodus.

David, the young hero who became a king, was not without faults. I knew he slew the giant Goliath with a stone and soon became the king of Israel. But I did not know that he had his imperfections. For instance, when David's men were out fighting battles, he should have been there in the thick of the battle with his men, but David remained in his palace. "But David remained at his palace one evening he got up from his bed and walked around on the roof of the palace. From the roof he saw a woman bathing. The woman was very beautiful and David sent someone to find out about her" (2 Sam. 11:2).

Imagine that after hearing about this great warrior and leader in my youth and now reading the Word and discovering David was a Peeping Tom! I believe men can relate to David as we struggle with guarding our eyes from what we focus on.

Imagine if David had the media and risqué publications that bombard us today. His failings did not stop there. He pursued this woman, and he impregnated her. Then he had her husband Uriah, his soldier, killed in war.

I would encourage new believers to read the books of Ruth and Esther in the Bible. These two women of the Bible had open minds and a heart for the Lord and proved that God uses the lives of biblical women to teach and inspire women today.

I have learned about the lives of other people in the Bible in both the Old and New Testaments who struggled with their fallen natures, and yet God used them for His glory. From the beginning to the end of the Bible, I have had a glimpse of personalities and failings in the accounts of these biblical figures. Adam and Eve were disobedient blame shifters. Jacob was a schemer. Joseph thought he was better than anyone else. He was a favorite son of Jacob and begrudged by his brothers. Moses made excuses and had a speech impediment. Saul was jealous of David. James, the half-brother of Jesus, was a skeptic who turned into a leader of the church based on his meeting with the resurrected Christ. Rahab was a prostitute but known for her great faith. This remarkable Gentile woman could lead deeper insights into God's plan for church and His dealing with individual believers in grace and mercy. Peter was impetuous to the point of acting in a rash manner. He is known for denying Jesus three times; however, Jesus forgave Peter and still used him for ministry and glory. The nameless Samaritan woman who came to draw water at the well had an encounter with Jesus. An unmarried woman had five men in her life. She was living an immoral life. She knew she was a sinner who needed to see herself as a person of worth and value. These true accounts teach us that God finds us worthy of His love in spite of our morally fallen lives.

I began to read the Bible just before my thirty-fourth birthday, and through my years of increasing faith, I have learned the character and natures of fallible men and women and God the Father and Christ the risen Savior. Now that my heart is open and available for God to use me, I'm getting close and personal with these men and women of fallen natures in the Bible whom God used for His glory. Their lives were blessed. In Sunday school, they taught me about the saints who were perfect people with halos around their heads who followed God. They did not teach me about Steven, the first martyr to give his life for the gospel.

Another important fact left out was about Saul of Tarsus, who violently persecuted Christians. He was a Pharisee who held the law and came against Christians because he believed he was doing God's work. Then he became the apostle Paul, one of the greatest messengers of the gospel after his Damascus Road encounter with Christ.

Now the account of Judas betraying Jesus, I remember from my youth before I read the Bible. I don't know why only that true personal account was revealed. I believe the Bible is true because of the way it truthfully describes the human condition. A person, a close friend, may lie right to our face, and then when our back is turned, he or she curses us. We are dazed in disbelief that this person we trusted could turn on us. The Bible reveals the truth about the source of this behavior and our fallen sinful nature, but God loves creations. And we are His, and He created a solution. Man alone cannot do that. With mankind, we will always have to pays a price. But in order to grant us redemption, God gave up His only Son so we can choose to be with Him in eternity. I read about the struggles these men and women faced, and although the clothes and technology have changed dramatically, our human behavior has not.

The Trinity is difficult to understand, The Father, The Son, and The Holy Spirit. A believer needs to have a heavenly understanding. My mother and I had a discussion recently on how we can come to a human understanding how the Trinity works. Quite a few people have asked me how is it possible for believers to worship the Father, The Son, and The Holy Spirit. Wouldn't that make three gods instead of one God? God the Father, Jesus the Son, and The Holy Spirit are one, how can this be without having three separate worshipped entities. My mother in her wisdom came up with a way to help understanding in our earthly logic. We all know about the element water. In liquid stage it is known as H2o, aqua, water. Freeze a container of water and it becomes ice. Place a pot of water on the stove and as it boils it becomes steam. I don't know everything about God but I do understand how water changes its nature. God created bodies of water. If water can be one element in three stages it is possible that God the Father, Jesus the Son, and The Holy spirit can be one in three. It can also be looked at this way; The Father and Son are on Their Throne and their Holy Spirit is the fog that surrounds us. The choice is ours either we receive it or we don't.

At times, I have difficulty understanding and comprehending what I just read. When that happens, I read through it and pray the Lord will give me an understanding. Other times, I will be reading during a difficult time, and that particular verse covers a life issue I'm dealing with. The Word speaks clearly. I didn't like some parts of the Bible at first, especially when it speaks of conviction sin and I know what I'm being called on. But unlike mankind, God has a forgiving nature, and through the Word, I can come into God's presence and receive His forgiveness. My wisdom increases more and more from the Word of God, and I have learned from my past mistakes, which my sin and own disobedience to God caused. Having the conscience of a loving, caring, and involved dad, I can imagine how it must grieve God when His children don't listen and get hurt from an action that appeared innocent at the time. I have warned my daughter about the careless and distracted drivers who cruise through parking lots with no regard of safety to pedestrians. A parent's biggest fear is a child's mortal mistake in a world full of people who are careless and irresponsible.

God did not create us to be conforming mindless beings wandering aimlessly through a dull, lifeless existence. We were created with a free will and ability to make decisions. We reach an age where we can distinguish right from wrong. Sometimes we know that certain actions will cause pain, but we become rebellious and ignore the consequences that cause pain. The Bible explains why we struggle in life. Our problems began in the garden of Eden with a rebellious decision and has continued through our present time. We struggle with our insatiable flesh, and the only way to conquer self-centeredness is to focus on God. Our problems and conflicts with other people are of a spiritual nature. The only way to understand this spirit of opposition is made known to us through the Word of God. Despite this opposing spiritual difficulty we have inherited, we can have a better understanding of humanity and our Creator. God teaches us through His Word when we read and shows us in true story accounts failed human nature that we can relate to.

The Bible is not just a reading tool. It is the living Word of

God and guides us through problems we face in life. He speaks to us through His Word as long as we have a humble nature and are willing to hear His wisdom. This topic on the Bible and the question whether it is true and trustworthy is full, profuse in arguments and discussions. Is the Bible just a mythical book for silly Pollyanna people to dream about a heaven and determine whether that heaven really exists?

When I came to a point in my life with a sense of being empty and alone, I came to the cross. Although I was skeptical when I entered that born-again church in 2001, I was available to listen and make my own choice. Once I made that decision, God put me through some life situations to show me how stubborn and prideful I can be. But God, unlike man, has a no-fail solution, and that was and is through His Son. When man has a solution, it usually costs somebody something. For God, it costs Him the suffering and agony to His risen Son so we don't have to pay for our sins and failures. The innocent Son of God suffered for all sons and daughters, and soon we will be resurrected for our reunion and final home. The Bible is God's authoritative Word, and it has never changed in showing human behavior. The Word shows people who pleased God despite their failed nature and people who displeased God and chose to be grounded to earthly pleasures. The Bible is numerous books bound in heavenly understanding.

In order to understand this book, that is, in order to understand God, we must be heavenly minded, or our earthly minded logic will blind us from God's truth. People continue to pass off the Word of God in this relentless act of rebellion with a barrage of arguments and denial. Despite this opposition against God, His Word, and His Son, the Bible has not and will not change. These times and truths the Bible foretells will occur whether we accept it or not. The Word of God has withstood time unlike any book of ancient or present time. It is as provocative today as it was when it was first written. Ever since I have been studying the Word, I have gained a sense of awareness of this great planet that God breathed life into.

Three days before writing this sentence in the fall, I was cleaning my windows. I pulled one of the double-paned windows out of the sill to wipe it clean. I had my radio playing my Christian station. The music was pleasing to my ears. It must have been pleasing to the ears of my visitor, who came to my screen unannounced. Out of the corner of my eye, I observed movement of a three- to four-inch green creature of God walking on the outside screen of the screen. It was a praying mantis, and I briefly halted my cleaning while I observed this beautiful insect. It moved slow and graciously, as if it were listening to the music glorifying its designer. I took a picture of it on my phone, and then quietly and without disturbing the screen it was resting on, I placed my windows back onto the tracks. I viewed the pictures I took, which were crisp and clear despite the obstructed view of the screen window. I looked closely at the features of this insect. Its "hands" appeared to be in "praying formation." The grasslike green color of the insect makes it possible to hide from its predators, looking like a blade of grass. The mantis' legs had the appearance of small limbs of a sprouting plant. I marveled at the beauty, grace, and design of this crawling creature.

Another design of God's creation enters my mind just as beautiful as this insect, but it is not an insect. It is the natural weather wonder that occurs during a rainstorm when the sun shines through a summer storm cloud and a rainbow glows if only for a brief moment. What baffles me is supposedly evolution is responsible for all these earthly wonders, which happens by chance. It just doesn't make sense to me that, one day, "bang" all of this happened. It boils down to personal belief. Either we believe what the Bible says or we don't, even though the evidence in all its mystery and beauty is there revealed to us in God's Word.

I have been in my walk of faith for a decade, and something that boggles my mind and perhaps this problem answers the reason why some Christians are pompous hypocrites. How can someone calling himself or herself a Christian live a Bible-believing life, which is what our faith is about, when he or she is not in the Word. How can we have passion for our faith and toward humanity when we are not reading the ultimate book of passion? The Bible speaks to us who God is and what His nature is, but how can a believer have understanding and passion for God and all that He is unless we study His Word? If we don't know and love the Bible, how can we know and love God?

Pastor Lou counseled me and encouraged me to read some difficult verses. No matter what mixed feelings I have over certain convicting verses, God loves me, and He shows it by redemptive verses that are a kiss from His lips. Through His Word, He tells me how much He wants to restore my life. I was grateful to read what God did for me through His Son when I first became a believer. At the same time, the verse that describes our good works to earn His grace like filthy rags troubled me. I never heard that before. I was always taught that, after I sinned, I was to go to confession and be redeemed. After that, I would continue to do my good deeds, answer volunteer fire calls, help the old lady cross the street, and so forth. I performed my good deeds to be a virtuous person and earn my entrance into heaven. We are deceived that our good works will cover our bad actions as sinners, but only God through His Son Jesus Christ can redeem us and remove the filth of our past. Maybe so many believers backslide and fail in their ability to witness and serve others because they have no idea or understanding of how their new life in Christ is to be lived.

I mentioned earlier making an ambitious attempt to read the Bible all the way through in a year's time. I wanted to be able to say that I had read the entire Word of God. Then I received some very good wisdom on this theory of mine in a Sunday morning life lesson at my church. Getting the Bible in your head is not as important or effective as getting it in your heart. The Word of God should spiritually feed you and lead you during a personal crisis. Whatever you are facing, there are verses for every problem we face, and scriptures that pertain to your situation will give you hope through your problem. Whatever your problem may be, you will get the best help and hope through the Word. Most Bibles have an index to verses that give you hope and encouragement on different areas of struggle, such as, for example, worry, fear, stress, betrayal, conflict, and so forth. World philosophy deals with one's own inner strength to conquer problems. But our problems are of a spiritual matter; only God can provide us divine answers and healing in our problems. It is good to read and discover the personal accounts of men and women in the Bible.

Now I have heard some folks say they cannot relate to that Bible stuff because it was so long ago that people and times have changed. The times and language have changed, but human behavior remains the same. Depending on where you are in life, the Word of God will speak to you, providing you read and allow yourself to be open and available to what His

Word has to say. It is a personal spiritual hunger to find hope, healing, and purpose that drives a person to seek hope and truth, a belief we were meant to be more in life than just living every day as the same old life, just a different day. If life gives us dung, we can turn it into fertilizer and have a beautiful and bountiful garden. In agriculture, healthy seeds can grow into fruitful produce from cow manure.

One year when I was living at my parents' house, I planted a garden with various vegetables. I took some cow manure and blended it into the earth I tilled with my tractor. My dad and I harvested the best corn on the cob we ever tasted, fond memories of gardening with my father.

Getting back to Bible reading, there are times when I have difficulty understanding what I just read. But then there are other times when I'm going through a personal conflict that I am comforted. I recall opening my Bible at random one day and seeking guidance in a trial I was going through that had me frustrated. The page I turned to was a verse on forgiveness. I was dealing with a person whom I had severe personal conflict with. I didn't know what to pray for. I just wanted cooperation with this person. God spoke to my heart in this scripture on forgiveness. I decided I would change my behavior and not take this person's insults to heart. I suppose that this person had animosity toward certain people in his or her life and he or she needed a scapegoat. I was placed in that position. I changed my attitude toward this irritating person.

When we have irritating people in our lives, we may want to wish they go away. When we think that way, someone else with the same sandpaper personality that conflicts with ours replaces those irritating people. God has shown me that we cannot change people or their behavior, but we can adjust our attitude toward them. When we realize this, we learn to interact with conflicting people and remain in control of our own behaviors. I now understand that many people with irritating personalities will enter my life. But I have the wisdom and ability to control my attitude and my behavior. I have also learned not to allow abrasive people to control me. I try to put myself in other people's shoes. There must be a reason why these behavior problems exist in people. In my observations of human behavior, I have found that personality problems in a person may be inherited from parents or an unbalanced family childhood, such as growing up in a mentally or physically abusive home. It makes sense to me that a person who never received love, guidance, and affection in childhood becomes an adult who seeks attention by acting in a grinding and disturbing behavior. When we are required to interact with people of disturbing personality disorders, we must understand and not take their irritating behavior personally. In some cases, it may be that a person is carrying toxic emotional baggage from his or her past on his or her back and looking for someone to dump it on. We can choose not to receive this in our minds by telling ourselves, "I don't receive this toxic behavior."

We can also pray for that person who causes us irritation. Of course, I could act out my anger brought on by this troubled person, but that's exactly what the enemy of my faith wants me to do. It pleases God that I pray for those who come against me, and I have developed this lifestyle through faith. Some people who have a sour and bitter outlook on life may be in personal, mental, and spiritual pain. Perhaps they don't seek help because of pride or fear. The Bible has the spiritual antidote for pride and fear in us, and that is placing our trust in Christ. In a situation of mental illness, a person should seek professional help.

This person in my life that I spoke of earlier seemed to believe that life dealt him or her lemons, and he or she had to share his or her sourness with everyone he or she encountered. I decided to change my behavior, and I would not play hot potato with this toxic behavior and carry it in my own life. There are plenty of people with an abundant supply of toxic thought and stinking thinking, and they want to give you the overflow of their gloomy views of life. There is joy in the Lord. Receive it. Forgive these people. They may not realize the problem. When you receive toxic behavior from someone, ask the Lord to take it away and fill you with forgiveness.

I often use the term "believer" in this book to describe a follower of Christ instead of using Christian. In my point of view, there is a significant difference between calling oneself a believer and a Christian. Calling ourselves Christians does not necessarily imply that we are believers in the Word of God. Believers read the Word and show the Bible through actions of serving other people, whether it be physical needs or prayer.

I remember some past news headlines where people claiming to be Christians were caught in acts of violence and misinterpreting the Bible, claiming their acts in the name of God. The only acts that can be claimed in the name of Christ are acts of love because Jesus is love. Except for some celebrities who are believers, I haven't noticed ordinary believing citizens making news coverage for praying over other people in public or showing the love of Christ by serving people in acts of kindness. Usually the media captures misguided individuals whose passion for their belief turns against them, and they act as the judge of the Word of God instead of following the spirit of Christ and going into prayer. When we read the Bible as scholars, we develop a Pharisaical pride and often become the judge and jury and cast judgment of guilt over other people.

What is a believer to do when concerned about other people who are not living a life honoring God? An act of violence is not a Christlike character. Nowhere in the Bible have I read where Jesus held signs of hatred, spoke harshly, or acted in violence. Jesus spoke gently but with authority over those who were in sin. He spoke harshly to the Pharisees who walked in judgment and hypocrisy. The only act of violence in Jesus life was when He was crucified on the cross. He did not go along the roadside speaking harsh words against people who lived unholy lives. He did tell people the truth of the consequences of their sinful actions. Jesus condemned the actions of unholy people but spoke love to the people. In John 8, a woman is caught in adultery, and the teachers of the law and the Pharisees were about to stone her to death.

But Jesus said to them, "If any of you is without sin, let him be the first to throw a stone at her."

They left, leaving only Jesus and the woman in the yard.

Jesus said to her, "Woman, where are they? Has no one condemned you?"

"No, sir," she said. "Then neither do I condemn you."

Jesus declared, "Go now and leave your life of sin."

Another example is when the Pharisees asked Jesus why His disciples did not traditionally cleanse their hands before they eat. "Listen to me everyone and understand this. Nothing outside a man can make him unclean by going into him. Rather it is what comes out of a man that makes him unclean" (Mark 7:14–16).

Here, Jesus spoke in love against hateful words that come from our mouths. In order to live a life of faith through our actions, prayer is essential in keeping us in tune with God. Jesus depended on communication to His Father through prayer, and we, as His followers, must do the same. Only our prayers for lost and hurting people will bring the love of God into people's lives. Silent prayer is the best act of love a believing Christian can perform. Jesus was and is the ultimate prayer warrior. Most warriors wield a sword or weapon. Prayer and the Word of God were the weapons Jesus used against the forces of darkness and evil. Look how He prayed in the garden of Gethsemane in Matthew 26:36–46. When Jesus prayed to God the Father, if there any alternative to His sacrifice, He prayed so hard and diligently that His sweat became blood. Now I'm not saying that we will begin to sweat blood if we pray hard enough. The point is that believers who live for the Lord need to focus our energy and passion of our faith in the same lifestyle that Jesus did. He healed people and taught them about the love of the Father. His death saved us, and His resurrection promises that we who believe in Him will be resurrected and spend eternity with Him. We are to reach out to lost and hurting people, those who are looking for truth. They want to know what we have is real. I believe that is the reason for our trials. People observe our hardships, and they are baffled at how we can have such joy during a painful period. We can share hard times with people and introduce Jesus Christ as the source of our joy and redemption. If we are going to be servants for Jesus, we have to be in the Word of God. We have to be prayed up and available. God is not looking for perfection. He is looking for brokenhearted people who can heal other despairing people and love God and people, no matter what.

There is a misconception that the church and its leaders give strict hard-line rules and regulations. The church tells believing Christians what we can and cannot do in life. In a church that teaches the gospel, we find our life instructions for living an abundant life through Christ in the Bible. The first commandment we have is that we shall have no other gods before us; nor shall we make any image our god. He is the only living God who gave us hope of eternal life through the sacrifice of His Son and resurrecting Him from the dead. Our standards of living are based on biblical principles of living.

Someone once asked me if my church tells me who to vote for during election time, and the answer is no. I research information on the running candidate's policies and beliefs. My personal choice in electing a candidate are those who protect our pledge of allegiance as one nation under God, support pro-life issues, and give support to husbands and wives for stronger marriages and families. I want a candidate who supports creation education for our children. Political parties do not persuade my decision. I am concerned about the individual candidate and want to know if he or she will represent my voice in key issues.

I have also been asked about my sobriety. Did I quit drinking because the church told me to? Well, the church had nothing to do with that decision. I did not choose sobriety until a year after walking in faith when my daughter was born. I made that choice so my daughter would have a better childhood with a dad who is dedicated to watching his child grow up through sober eyes. I also realized that reaching others with the good news of salvation is not very effective when you hold the Bible in one hand and a bottle of booze in the other. I'll have a toast to the rapture, but I don't want to be drunk when that blessed event happens.

Believers live by the life instructions of the Bible, not church rules or laws. The Bible will never deceive anyone. God made rules for our way of living for the same reason we make rules for our children. God made His rules out of love and protection for us from actions that will harm us. Mankind, however, often makes rules and regulations for personal power, which is usually self-guided and uncontrolled.

Someone asked me a question about foods. This person thought that, because I was extremely religious, I must have a strict dietary regimen. I had studied this topic prior to this conversation so I was able to explain this misunderstanding. In Mark 7:14–16, as noted in the latter part of this chapter, Jesus declared all foods acceptable to eat. The teachers of the Old Testament maintained these laws were originally written for proper reverence and living to God. However, these laws became tradition among the chief priests and teachers, contrary to God's reason for establishing them. Jesus declared the proper way to live through His instruction in the Bible, and the church body lives by that standard. We live by Christ, not religious tradition. Rules or regulations do not save us. The grace of God saves us through the sacrifice of His Son Jesus Christ. Our bodies are temples for our Father and Savior spirit to reside in. Our bodies were created to live and glorify God. The foods we eat should be nutritious and nourishing. Most of us like the foods that are not so healthy, like fried foods and baked sweet goods. I'm sure God is not against us having a sweet tooth as long as we eat certain foods not included in the healthy list in moderation. An occasional candy bar is okay, but our teeth were not designed for excessive sugar consumption, and neither are our bodies in such medical cases of diabetes.

Santa Claus

While doing my research in the Bible for the latter issues, I came up with some provocative topics, including the existence of Santa Claus. My nine-year-old daughter unexpectedly asked me this question. We were sitting at our dining room table. I was working on this book, and she was sitting across from me, working on her own projects. When her question suddenly rolled out of her mouth, I was stopped right in my tracks.

She asked with innocence and curiosity, "Daddy, is Santa Claus real?"

At that moment, I felt like a boxer being cornered in the ring with two options: punch my way out of this situation with truth or take the hit and lie. Actually for a parent, this question places us in an awkward position. Santa Claus is a mythical figure and legend who, in many Western cultures, is believed to bring gifts to the homes of the good children during the late evening and overnight hours of Christmas Eve. However, a real man known as Saint Nicolas, possibly a priest who existed in history, did bring presents to poor children. Whether this man made a list of good and bad children, I do not know. Remember as a child we were told that Santa would bring us presents if we were good? The Easter bunny would leave a basket of goodies, and the tooth fairy would take our tooth from our pillow and leave some money. Then before our teen years, most of us found out on our own that none of these mythical characters ever existed. When we were children, we believed them to be real because we were told they were real. Perhaps you felt an emotional disappointment when finding out that what you believed to be real in your childhood never existed. Yet we are brought to church and told that God and Jesus Christ exist, but we have never witnessed their physical presence in our lifetime.

So what do you believe in when you discover that whom you believed in as a child was actually an ordinary mortal person acting out these fabled characters? You may wonder about God,

Jesus Christ, and this place called heaven. Is it a real place or another man-created fable? What about this book called the Bible? Does anyone read this ancient text? Our minds are truly battlefields. One army is truth; the other army is lies. Which army will conquer our minds?

So how did I answer my daughter's question? I said a split-second silent prayer to myself that the Lord would let His words come out of my mouth.

I took a deep breath, looked her gently in her eyes, and replied with confidence, "Sweetheart, if Santa is in the Bible, then he is real."

I was amazed when she returned with, "Daddy, I don't think Santa is in the Bible, but the Bible says that Jesus is real."

I said, "Yes, Jesus is real, and He gave us our true gift."

At first, she showed signs of being let down about Santa. But when we talked about Jesus, she perked right up again, and our conversation went on to another topic. But the latter discussion is indelibly in my mind. I considered the sharp reactions I may receive from my adult peers when they find out my talk with my daughter. As a parent, it is my duty to be a role model seeking truth. I didn't just tell her. She asked her dad a question, expecting a truthful answer. So if I receive condemnation from other adults about what I teach my daughter based on the Word of God, so be it. I have developed an understanding of how God works, although I am only a neophyte theologian and have much more to learn. If people do get upset with me concerning my parenting through faith, then they probably don't have a heavenly understanding. I don't understand everything, and that's where having faith and trust is a must. I can rest at night knowing I rely on the Word of God for truth. The Bible says it, and I believe it.

We still celebrate Christmas because it is Jesus' birthday. Many adults don't believe in the Bible or the truth of God's Word. Perhaps they are the children who were told of childhood legends and fables and they believed these stories to be real in their young minds. The Bible is God's message that He does exist.

Aliens

This one is different from Santa Claus in that no one to my knowledge is trying to prove Santa is real except for movies. However, people are trying to prove the existence of aliens in the Bible. I have viewed television programs and listened to other people's theories on alien existence. One fact I have found in the Bible is that the Word repeats itself. The Word of God never contradicts itself. The book speaks of what God created. These creations include (and I'm paraphrasing) the earth, light, water, vegetation, animals, and crawling creatures. Then God created man to rule over the fish of the sea, the birds of the air, and every living thing that moves on the ground. "So God created man in his own image, in the image of God he created him; male and female he created them" (Gen. 1:27).

After this, there is no mention of another planet given breath by God; nor is there any other being beside Adam and Eve who was given life. God does not and cannot lie. There is nothing he cannot disclose to us for any reason. We may not understand His ways, but He withholds absolutely nothing from us. So why are we so adamant about proving aliens in the Bible? It goes back to the garden. God created Adam and Eve with the will to choose. Eve chose to listen to the serpent and eat of the apple; Adam did not help us men out either. We were given a free will to choose, but we chose rebellion that directs our attention away from God.

I have had discussions with nonbelieving men who are familiar with the Bible from a television perspective. They are led to believe that the Bible speaks of aliens. If there were other beings other than human beings, God would have made it crystal clear in the Bible. There is much discussion and confusion about the book of Ezekiel in the Bible. The description of the prophet's vision in Ezekiel 10 has caused quite a stir in modern man. Did the prophet Ezekiel witness an unidentified flying object or alien creatures? Did God present Himself as an alien being? In the prophet's time, there was a spirit of reverence for the God of heaven. Not only did men in those times have reverence, they had a heart for God to follow His will. They had great belief and respect for God's Word, along with who God was. They were not perfect, but they were open to His Word and made themselves available to serve Him. They were able to receive great visions like that in which Ezekiel wrote about. These men lived for God; therefore, they were available to see these visions.

Modern man has become extremely irreverent and rebellious toward God. Two men can read the Bible. One can choose to give reverence and availability to serve God. The other can choose to try to dethrone God of His existence and deny the truth of the Bible. God can never be dethroned; nor will the truth be denied. According to reverent prophets, Jesus appeared in a vision to give Ezekiel the message of repentance and redemption. In that vision were the living creatures called "cherubim," throne attendants representing God's creation. Man is God's ordained ruler of creation. The lion is the strongest of the wild beast. The ox is the most powerful of the domesticated animals, and the eagle is the mightiest of the birds. These four creatures appear again in Revelation 4:7 and are often seen in the paintings and sculpture of the Middle Ages where they represent the four gospels. The imagery of the intersecting wheels symbolizes the omnipresence of God. The eyes in the description of these wheels symbolize God's all-seeing nature. God is conveying a message that only a reverent man with a heart and understanding for God can understand. A wavering and rebellious man will look at this description and attempt to disprove the deity of God, that God presents Himself as an alien being. God is God, not an alien being, and heaven is a place, not a planet.

Sasquatch (Bigfoot)

There has long been a quest to prove that Bigfoot half-man and half-beast exists. What is the urgency in proving this myth a reality? Have you ever noticed the pictures taken of the half-man/half-beast are always fuzzy, just like UFO pictures? We never see pictures of aliens waving from their ships or clear pictures of Bigfoot and his family out and about. Is it possible that, if this half-man/half-beast could be proven to exist, then evolution is correct and creation and design are wrong? If evidence of Bigfoot exists today, it will prove we evolved from apes and were not created and designed by God. Therefore, if evolution is proved true, then God does not exist. The evolution theory is that we just happened and that we were not created and designed by God. But the Bible tells us that God created us. The book of Genesis reveals God's creation and design; therefore, we have been beautifully created and designed.

The Rapture

The Bible speaks of a moment in future time that only God knows when His Son Jesus Christ will descend from heaven just above the earth and gather all believers. Those who are living a life pleasing to God and have received Christ as their personal savior will be brought home in heaven for eternity. The Word of God describes this event in the book of Revelation, and it will happen only once. That is why a repentant life is so urgent. I remember back in the 1970s hearing about Jesus coming again and the rapture. I would see signs and bumper stickers that declared repentance before the coming of the rapture. I believe at least one movie has been made mocking the deity of Christ and the rapture.

So many people ask the question, "So when is Jesus coming back, and why is it taking so long?"

If Jesus can eradicate all evil once and for all, why does He not do it now? I have pondered these mysteries myself. I learn something new every day, and I don't have all the answers, but I am very observant of these matters. The Bible speaks of the rapture as a one-time event in the history of man. The rapture of believers will occur only one time. Whatever choice we have made is the final choice for us. I don't believe it is taking an extremely long time for the rapture to take place. I am convinced of God's love for us. He's not mad at us. He is mad about us. He does not want any of His children to perish. We have many chances to make a decision to receive Christ and turn our life around, but not much time is left. The Bible states that Jesus came to the earth to fulfill His command. He lived on the earth among mankind in human flesh to teach the gospel. He sacrificed His life for us, so when our physical bodies perish, we will be resurrected just as Jesus was and become spiritual beings. We will live in eternity with Him. He came the first time to bring the good news of God's love and to be our entrance into heaven, and mankind denied him. His second coming will be without warning or notice. The Lord will gather those who know Him as Savior and are living a life pleasing to Him, and it will happen "in the twinkling of an eye."

When the rapture is complete, there will be those who continue to deny Christ's deity. Perhaps some will still not believe in this rapture that just occurred. Chaos, confusion, and terrifying uncertain times unlike any other in history will unfold. Populations and cultures of people will have vanished without explanation. There will have to be some logical reason as to what happened to these people that just vanished out of thin air. If there is no God and no Messiah Jesus Christ, then where did all these missing people, including loved ones, go? What logical earthly explanation is there? Maybe the alien theory will be placed in action. Perhaps there are those who believe God and Jesus Christ are alien beings, and those crazy people called born-again Christians were actually alien beings among us in disguise. This may sound farfetched now, but when that moment happens, thoughts may radically change.

One event in our time evoked an image of what disasters might occur after the rapture is September 11, 2001. I remember where I was that morning and exactly what I did. We took a coffee break at work, and I offered to get the coffee list. I drove off and headed for the coffee shop. The radio was tuned to a top forty hits station when the new broke out on the airwaves. At that time, it was reported that the first plane had hit one of the towers in New York. My first thought was maybe a new pilot in a small plane made a tragic mistake. I took my time getting back because I was listening to the broadcast intently. When I heard the second tower, I immediately began praying to God. I had just become a believer in Christ in January of that year, and I believed that the best action I could take at that moment was prayer. The city is less than two hours south of where I live and grew up. Any home or business with a television set had people watching with concern over this alarming event.

When I came home that evening, I turned on the television and watched continuous coverage. By then, the news had confirmed the other crashes, the field in Shanksville, Pennsylvania, and the Pentagon. The destruction and chaos was unnerving. I watched as the news cameras showed ordinary American citizens taking heroic action, sacrificing their safety to save other people they didn't know. Civilians worked side by side with police officers and firefighters. American citizens dug in and helped no matter what the cost.

I talked to many people since that day, and the one question I hear is, "Where was God, and why did He allow this to happen?"

I am just an ordinary man with a heart for God. I am here to serve, pray, and show people the love of Christ. I am not an expert on God. God was in our schools. He was in our courts and public buildings. The Ten Commandments were taken out of public places. Prayer was taken out of school because it is offensive. What is so offensive about asking God in prayer to protect us from harm? Other gods are out there, but none protected us that day. God was kicked out of the city, but He did not totally remove Himself. He was there. He sent His people to rescue those in peril. Three hundred and forty-three firefighters made the ultimate sacrifice.

I am a former volunteer firefighter. When you're in a bad situation, you believe in something greater than you even if you're not deeply religious. Countless citizens came to each other's rescue, and some even died together when there was no escape. There are those who did not want God in the city, and they showed it by removing the Ten Commandments, prayer, and the Bible because it was too offensive. If the gods of this world cannot protect our lives and freedoms, our God in heaven will, and we need Him back! When ungodly acts of disaster are committed against our country, God is blamed for allowing it to happen. Prayer and a daily devotion will keep God close to us and enemies away. But when we tell God to leave, He is a gentleman, and so He does.

There is a dilemma. We want God's protection, but we don't want to live by His instruction, the guidelines of living that keep us from getting hurt in the first place. Despite mankind's will against God's presence, when everything is calm, God did answer prayers that day in the evidence of Americans doing what we always do when someone comes against our family. People weren't strangers that day. They were American citizens, family. That is exactly what happened on September 11. Someone came against the American family, and as dysfunctional a nation that we are, we came together as a family. Don't mess with our American family, and we won't mess with you.

According to the Word of God in the book of Revelation, there will be a catastrophic event, the rapture, a moment in time when followers of Christ will be swept in the arms of Christ. Believers, wherever they are at that time, will leave their workplaces, and vehicles will be unmanned. Planes will be without pilots. Whatever position a believer holds on this earth will be abandoned at that time. I witnessed unselfish men and women that September day.

But what will happen that day when Jesus brings His people home? Who will be left behind when destruction and chaos breaks out? Who will sacrifice their own lives to save others? What kind of people will there be who deny God and have no concern for human life other than their own? Most everyone is storing up for the end-times, but what happens when that supply runs out?

There is good news. We have a God who loves us and is crazy about us. He will never leave us, nor forsake us. But we need to make our own choice now and call upon God in the name of Jesus Christ. I have included some prayers that will help you in your time of need. I hope you will give them time as prayers need patience. If you have a difficult time reading the Bible, try saying these prayers, and give yourself some time. Don't pray in haste. Remember that prayer is having conversation with God. I encourage you to seek God in prayer, even if you are skeptical. Prayer has the power to work in your life, so try it. You have nothing to lose and everything to gain. God has abundant blessings stored up for your life, and He's waiting for you to ask for them. God is a gentleman and only enters your life with His abundant blessings if you let Him in your life. All you have to do is ask, believe, and receive.

One problem may cause a block in your prayer, unforgiveness. If you have unforgiveness in your heart, it is not worth holding onto and denying yourself what God wants you to have to fortify your life. Otherwise, the blessings you receive may turn into problems if you don't handle them the way God wants you to. Let God work in your life. He has a plan for your life, and He is waiting for you to open your heart and receive the life you were meant to have through His only Son, Jesus Christ. Don't wait any longer. In fact, put a bookmark in this page, and pray to God in Jesus' name for forgiveness and abundant blessings in your life. God can give you that which will not leave you empty.

Jesus said about prayer, "If you believe, you will receive whatever you ask for in prayer" (Matt. 21:22). So go ahead, put this book down, say your prayer, and then come back and read some prayers I have provided below.

"Our Father in heaven, Hallowed be your name, Your kingdom come, Your will be done on earth as it is in heaven. Give us today our daily bread. Forgive us our debts, As we also have forgiven our debtors. And lead us not into temptation, But deliver us from the evil one. For thine is the kingdom And the power and the glory For ever. Amen." (Matthew 6:9-13)

A very important verse follows this prayer. "For if you forgive men when they sin against you, your heavenly Father will also forgive you. But if you do not forgive men their sins, your Father will not forgive your sins" (Matt. 6:14). Receiving forgiveness and forgiving someone is vital if you want your prayers answered and abundant blessings poured onto you.

This next prayer, the Prayer of Jabez, is very brief but very powerful. "Oh God, that you would bless me indeed and enlarge my territory! Let your hand be with me, and keep me from causing pain to others" (1 Chr. 4:10 [KJV]).

Jabez is remembered for a prayer request rather than a heroic act. In his prayer, he asked God to bless him, help him in his work, be with him in all he did, and keep him from all evil and harm. Jabez acknowledged God as the true center of his work. When we pray for God's blessing, we should also pray that he would take his rightful position as Lord over our work, family, leisure time, and life. When we obey Him in our daily responsibilities, we are living heroically. Jabez prayed specifically to be protected from harm and pain. We live in a fallen world filled with sin, and it is important to ask God to keep us safe from the unavoidable evil that comes our way. But we must also avoid evil motives, desires, and actions that begin with us. Therefore, not only must we seek God's protection from evil, we must also ask God to guard our thoughts and actions. We can put His protection to use by filling our minds with positive thoughts and attitudes.

Jesus said the following prayer in the garden of Gethsamane. "Abba, Father, everything is possible for you. Take this cup from me. Yet not what I will, but what you will" (Mark 14:36). Was Jesus trying to get out of His task? Jesus expressed His true feelings, but He did not deny or rebel against God's will. His desire was to do what God wanted. Jesus' prayer highlights the terrible suffering He had to endure an agony so much more magnified because He had to take the sins of the world. This "cup" was the agony of alienation from God the Father at the cross. The sinless Son of God took our sins, and He was separated for a while from God so we could be eternally saved.

You can meditate on the following verse in your time of need.

> The Lord is my shepherd, I shall not be in want. He makes me lie down in green pastures, He leads me beside quiet waters, He restores my soul. He guides me in paths of righteousness For His name sake. Even though I walk through the valley of the shadow of death I will fear n evil, For you are with me; Your rod and staff, They comfort me. You prepare a table before me In the presence of my enemies. You anoint my head with oil; My cup overflows. Surely goodness and love will Follow me all the days of my life, And I will dwell in the house of the Lord forever (Ps. 23).

The latter prayer is the most popular and overlooked prayer by many people who are looking for hope in their lives. Every day, whether we read the newspaper or view news broadcasts, uncertainty and insecurity bombards us. The Lord's Prayer is a special and powerful prayer for our time in our post-September 11 lives. Are you struggling with uncertainty, fear, or helplessness? Is your life motto, "Same old garbage; just a different day"? You can change your situation, but you must believe that God can work in your life. He is just waiting for you to welcome Him into your heart and your life. God is kind, loving, gentle, and forgiving, and He is alive!

Jesus prayed the following prayer for all who would follow Him. The twelve disciples were ordinary men of their society, but they were available for Christ, and He chose them for the task of spreading the good news of the gospel to others. If a person's heart is humble and open, he or she can receive forgiveness and salvation. For believers who are in the Word of God, it is an honor for God to use them to share the message of Christ with a friend, acquaintance, or stranger. There are Christians who misunderstand their mission and purpose and miss the opportunity of witnessing to others the message of hope. Our mission is to live for Christ and to glorify God in or lives. We must know what the Bible says about living our own lives if we are to be transformed by biblical living, along with how other people will be inspired. We believers are God's role models. People believe by seeing us. If they don't see Christ in us, they won't believe there is a Christ. The only way your friend or loved one will know the Bible is through us, the believers. Are we learning the Word? Are we living the Word? Be a winner for Christ. Read His Word.

Jesus prays for future believers.

> Father, I want those who you have given me to be with me where I am, and to see my glory, the glory you have

given me because you loved me before the creation of the world. Righteous Father, though the world does not know you, I know you and they know that you have sent me. I have made you known to them, and will continue to make you known in order that the love you have for me may be in them and that I myself may be in them (John 17:24–26).

The last part of that verse speaks volumes as to the influence of a believer toward others. By interacting with us, will the love of the Lord that overflows in us affect nonbelievers? To the believer, we carry the love of the Lord to others, and that love is shown through God's living Word. To the nonbeliever, there is unconditional love for your soul in the Bible. Don't give up! I pray you will know God's love through a believer who carries the Lord's love.

Chapter 6

The Divorced Parent

I performed some research for this subject and discovered some vital information about the creation of man and woman, marriage, and the existence of divorce. I studied the book of Genesis and followed up with online research as well as library information. God created man first and then the woman for companionship, and marriage was created. The fall of man created divorce. God acknowledges divorce and allows it in certain cases where abuse may exist. God loves marriage; He hates divorce. I believe that divorce happened when man disobeyed God and made his own choices and decisions. This study opened my eyes to what I never knew before. God knows what man needs. He provided Adam a companion in Eve, and He will provide modern man with our companion, but only if we focus on God. The death of marriage by divorce happened after the fall of man in the garden. It is a loss equivalent to losing a loved one because we have done just that. It brings life-changing difficulty when our children are involved. It is an ugly word, and it becomes an ugly situation when brought into legal action. Once the legal issues have been settled, you start to pick up the remainder of your life. You start to think about your new life change and chart a direction. If you are young and have no children, you may have better resiliency. However, if you are a divorced parent, the challenges ahead will test your physical, mental, and spiritual mettle. No one is exempt from this heartbreaking experience, not even Christians. Healing after this life-changing crisis takes time, for only time can heal emotional wounds. I prayed fervently during that time period against the spirit of unforgiveness and that I would make wiser decisions with a heart for pleasing God. When I accepted Christ as my personal Savior, I no longer went to bars or nightclubs, and I lost many friends because of my new lifestyle. Pastor Lou was my mentor, and through his influence, I chose to live a life that pleases God.

When my ex and I divorced, I lost more friends who did not agree with our decision. This was the point where I almost broke away from faith. I began writing some thoughts on paper to cope with this situation. You're afraid to talk to anyone, lest you feel like you're a crying burden on someone's shoulder. After the divorce was legally settled, I was on my way home from dropping off my daughter at her mother's one evening when emotion overcame me. The schedule of going back and forth from my home to my ex's was new and adding stress. I pulled my truck over and began yelling at God. (I don't suggest doing this. God deserves our reverence at all times.) He knew I was angry in this difficult situation. Everything came to a boiling point. As soon as I decided to walk with the Lord, I lost my "old friends." Everyone around me thinks I'm weird because I became a Jesus freak sharing the gospel, praying for people, and handing out Bible tracts. Now I'm dealing with being a divorced dad and all this traveling back and forth. I wanted to give up and leave this faith. In my old religion, I had friends.

Everyone liked being around me, and no one thought of me as a Bible freak. No one mocked my faith in Jesus Christ.

Then the Lord did what He does best. He played back the tape in my mind of how He has transformed me and He is not finished with me yet. I'm not a selfish drunk anymore. I am a sober, responsible dad. I'm not on a path of pleasurable desires of my flesh anymore. I'm praying for people with problems instead of making their problems worse by spreading gossip and slander about them. The book of Job came across my mind. He was tested beyond belief. Everything was taken away from him except for his life. I thought about my own life situation at that moment. Job lost much more than I did, and he still praised God.

I was still parked along the road in prayer, and I apologized to my heavenly Father for my anger and irreverent behavior. I instantly received a sense of calmness and peace around me. Jesus is my friend, and no matter who disagrees with me or does not stand by me, whether they are a believer or not, I know Jesus will never leave me because the Bible tells me so. My daughter decorated my life with living hues when it seemed everyone else tried to take away that beauty and color. I have faced many challenges as a divorced dad with my daughter.

Although I am writing this chapter from a divorced single father's point of view, we cannot forget about divorced single mothers who are in this post-divorce battle. A dad's task of providing a daughter's needs alone is challenging and difficult. To the mother of a son who is also alone in her task of providing needs, she is being challenged as well. Divorced parents need more support and counsel groups where they can connect with other divorced parents. We should not look down upon divorced parents, especially if people of faith are passing judgment. You don't need that. You need help and support.

I have the blessing of my mother in my life to help me with certain tasks only a woman can do with a girl. I did not always have that opportunity available when out in public and she needed a restroom. There have been quite a few times when I would take her out, just daddy-and-daughter time, and I would have to ask the assistance of another woman when dealing with bathroom issues. When my daughter was younger, I would try to select a grandmother type or a mother with children in tow. I also stood close by the bathroom door so she could hear me and know that all was secure.

One time, my mother, daughter, and I dined out at a buffet restaurant. My daughter was about seven, and I let her go by herself because she was gradually gaining her independence. I could see the bathroom door from our table. It seemed to have taken her some time when I asked my mother to check on her. Thank God she checked on her when she did. My mother entered the ladies' room of this restaurant and found four disrespectful teenagers harassing my seven-year-old daughter. My daughter heard them using inappropriate language. My daughter apparently commented to these girls that they shouldn't curse. I teach my daughter respect for people and proper civil conduct through her faith. Unfortunately, we live in an unrighteous and immoral world, and teenagers have no adult role models for civilized public conduct. My mother came to my daughter's rescue and attempted to reason with these poor, misguided teenagers that she was only a little girl. Then my mother escorted my daughter back to our table. A dad and mother never rest. They are always on watch!

Among the other challenges I faced were two different households where certain rules oppose each other. I have two rules in particular: abiding by "As for our household, we will serve the Lord" and eating dinner meals at the table as a family and saying grace. Often my daughter wants to eat at the living room table in front of the television because she is used to this. I have been firm in my stance on eating at the dinner table, and while it has been a long struggle, we do sit as a family even though it is just the two of us and we take turns saying grace. Often, my daughter will extend her dinnertime prayers, and it warms my heart to see her show consideration for others in prayer.

I also filter television shows and movies to ensure they are family friendly and free of potty language and sexual innuendos. I also encourage her to watch television shows and movies from an era when television and movies were child friendly. Television can be very mentally harmful and sexually suggestive to a child's mind, so an aware parent must filter and supervise these programs. I established my household by the order of my faith. "But as for me and my household, we will serve the Lord" (Josh. 24:15).

Despite my divorce, I will not let this painful, heartbreaking setback control my spiritual life nor my responsibilities as a father. I confessed my transgressions to the Lord in prayer and reconciled myself with God. As imperfect as I am, I want to be a believing role model for my daughter. I want her to witness that, no matter what life throws at us, as long as we seek the Lord with all our heart and our might, nothing can draw us away from the Lord our God unless we allow it.

I encourage divorced moms and dads to establish a decree in your home that yours will be one godly instruction. Divorce is a critical time in your walk with the Lord. You may not want to attend services in your current situation. Questions may fill your mind. "What will they say, and how will they see me in their eyes?" Remember that the church is God's house, not man's. If you feel you need to attend another place to worship the Lord, pray on it until you receive an answer. The Lord will speak to your heart. While you are waiting, keep in mind the purpose of attending church is to glorify God for who He is and what He has done, no matter what crisis we go through. We are also showing our children by example that we live by faith, we glorify God in our attendance, and we will not give up, no matter where we are in life. He is the same, and He will never leave us nor forsake us. He will carry us through our personal pain. A Christ-centered church will welcome you with open arms and a hug without judgment of your situation. However, if your situation is alcoholism or any other addictive or abusive behavior, that body of believers may reprove you out of love of Christ. You must leave that destructive lifestyle if you want to receive a life-changing transformation that is only possible through Jesus Christ. If you are struggling with problems of a spiritual nature, I suggest contacting an organization called Focus on the Family. This organization based on faith in Christ specializes in families, marriages, and people in crisis. Their website is www.focusonthefamily.com. They can help you.

Chapter 7

A Dream + A Written Plan x Action = Reality

This book was a dream. The thoughts and ideas for this book were in my mind, waiting to be born into action. I always had a knack for writing, but I never revealed it to anyone until I was asked to write a letter one day. Someone who gives the gift of encouraging words often inspire people. These words give a person the impetus he or she needs to take action and pursue an idea or dream. My inspiration to write a monumental project such as my first published book came from a most unusual source. You would not think an attorney could be inspirational, but mine was the exception.

I was going through some matters that required legal assistance. I was required to write a personal letter that the judge ruling over this case would read. I work in the construction field, although my employment is civil service. I knew I could not write the letter in laymen's words, which I speak quite often on the job if I desired my case to be taken seriously in court. So I wrote a rough draft, and then I revised it. My only help was a dictionary. Then I presented my letter to my legal counselor for review.

She first asked, "Did you have any help in writing the letter?"

I told her, "I used a dictionary to use the best words I could figure out to describe my situation with proper grammar."

Then I heard the most encouraging and inspiring word ever spoken to me since my grade school teacher who spent an entire day teaching me multiplication. My attorney, Lisa E. Hartley, described my letter as being written eloquently. She also added nice work. Her compliment was brief and direct but a very effective statement. When she spoke that word "eloquent," it did something to me that, when I came home that night, I looked over the first ten pages I wrote to start a book. On those ten pages, I wrote all my anger and frustration over my situation at the time.

When I read these pages in my calm, ease state of mind, I asked myself, "Who would want to read this angry garbage? What is my faith about? Is it anger and revenge, or is it of love, forgiveness, and redemption?"

I shredded those self-centered pity pages and began to write a book of witness and hope. I read somewhere that, if you have unforgiveness and anger toward a person and you cannot personally approach him or her, one of the best ways to get this personal garbage out of your heart is to write it on paper. Write every angry word that has taken residence in your heart and controlled your life. When you are done, immediately put that letter in the shredder or your fireplace, or dispose of it so a soul can never read it again. Destroy it! I tried this suggestion, and it has worked for me. All of that selfish, bitter, angry junk that was stored in my heart is now destroyed with that paper. This act of writing an angry letter and destroying it is a symbolic way of taking those words and toxic emotions in my heart and destroying them forever.

Anger and unforgiveness can steal your life away. Anger is natural and normal, but if not dealt with properly, it leads to unforgiveness and angry revenge and will harm you, physically and spiritually. In certain cases, however, professionally counseling may be required for serious physiological issues.

Once I received my inspiration to become a writer, I decided to take a brief vacation to Myrtle Beach, South Carolina. I had other destination options, but I talked to some friends, and they gave Myrtle Beach rave reviews. I had never traveled to the South before, so I set plans for the beach. I took a lone cruise in my pickup truck and drove straight through on a twelve-hour trip. It took me fourteen hours on my overnight drive because I did not realize my GPS system gives traveling options to the owner. Yes, I suppose I could have read the instructions; however, I consider myself an explorer. I chose a night trip, thinking I would have less traffic to deal with and I would make good timing. I discovered on this trip anyway that there was no difference in night and day because there was still delivery traffic. But the night traffic heavy in urban areas continued to flow without delay.

Once I arrived at the hotel on this sunny summer morning, the sight of the beautiful Southern beach welcomed me. The oceanic atmosphere and Southern hospitality of the South Carolina folks was just the calming, relaxed environment a burgeoning writer needs. The hotel where I stayed had a breakfast buffet of Southern delight. Every morning, I went downstairs to the dining area where the aroma of pancakes, sausage, bacon, and scrambled eggs, among other delights, filled my nostrils. My taste buds were greeted with pleasing nourishment as well as delicious seasonings. My schedule consisted of waking in the morning to the natural euphoric scenery of sand and ocean water topped with whitecaps that took my breath away from my balcony view.

After having my morning nourishment, I set out for the beach that was only a few footsteps from behind the hotel. The first day, I observed a machine traveling slowly up and down the sandy beach. I realized that this city-operated machine was combing the sand of debris, and when he was done, the sandy paradise was immaculate. I walked the beach in the morning, searching for seashells to bring back home to my daughter. In the afternoon, I lounged on my blanket and gazed at the graceful horizon, noting to myself how the water and sky met. I was born and raised in upstate suburban New York, and although we have beaches in New York, I did not see the ocean much, at least not an experience like Myrtle Beach.

I continued working on this book with refreshing insight and a new direction. I jotted down my thoughts on paper and put them in bullet points. I would then extend those points into sentences. Those sentences were placed into paragraphs, which were then arranged according to the order of that topic. An subject idea came to me on the power of our spoken words. According to the Bible (and I believe this to be true), our words come from our hearts. The words we speak have power, and the spoken word cannot be taken back. That is why we must think before we speak.

Before I proceed further, I'm not talking about speaking politically correct. My father was a school bus driver. Our family did not call him a public school transportation specialist. Dad was a bus driver, and he took pride in what he did. I'm talking about having a conversation with someone who has a gloomy outlook on life, the kind of person who grounds your joyful optimism with toxic opinions and puts dismal words that produce self-doubt. People with this shallow perspective will tell you that dreams are nice but you have to face reality. But look at how many people changed reality with their ideas, especially in this age of technology. Daily cell phone use and texting was not a reality fifty years ago. Before Thomas Edison invented the lightbulb, electricity was not a reality for early Americans. What do we know about a person's dreams and inventive creativity that we can give him or her our dash of reality and opinions? We who have dreams and imagination cannot control the gray cloud that people cast on our brilliant resourcefulness. We can control what goes into our minds by accepting messages that help and inspire us and deleting those messages that will destroy our attempts to believe and reach our goals. I don't receive "can't do thinking"; I only receive "can do thinking through well thought" organized solutions. Whenever I sense that someone speaks thoughts of gloom and dismal days ahead, I quietly tell myself that I don't receive that hopeless message. Some people go by a farm, and their nose turns in disgust at the odor of the pungent country air of cow manure, but I smell the vital ingredient for a wondrous bounty of fruits and vegetables bursting with vibrant, natural flavor.

Have you ever asked someone how his or her life is going? Occasionally, someone will reply "Ah, same old stuff. Just a different day." I refuse to view life with such mediocrity. When I decided to pursue writing, I changed my direction. I have a written plan and goals I'm aiming for, so I have set sail for victory!

After my exhilarating and rested days in that warm, bright, sandy paradise with the background of the serene ocean, I was now ready to write a book of encouragement, inspiration, and spiritual survival. My mind was now charged with inspiration and ambition to pursue a writing dream by having a written plan and set goals. I started reading books on writing and grammar because I didn't have the finances for college or the time, so I made due with books from my favorite bookstore and studying at home. The most important investment for me was reading time, learning about well-known authors, like how they started and what they recommend to those who wish to write. I don't know these authors personally, but I do feel close to them as a writer through their books.

This book has been in the making five years with the last two spent in four revisions. I have had many days of frustration and physical fatigue from a day's work responsibilities and being a responsible son to my mother and a reliable father to my daughter. I have always managed to construct ideas and subjects on paper and the message of what I want to convey to my reader. I have maintained my writing strength to continue forward to my goal by the grace of God.

At a point during the five revisions, I almost thought about giving up. I didn't seem like I was getting anywhere, and then I took a brief pause, drew a deep breath, and looked at the pages I had accomplished. I prayed and talked myself through this difficulty while listening to Zig Ziglar, a popular motivational speaker with a deep faith in Christ.

I thought to myself, "I have come so far."

I realized I had written sixty-three pages at that time, and the pages were expanding with more insight. Just like building a house, my book had structure. I only needed to paint and add furniture. To alleviate the pressure associated with writing, I'll take breaks, go for walks, and observe life and people in motion. I'll read various books on the writing process and author biographies. I'm learning as a writer that revising a book is a wonderful opportunity to write my book with improvement, and it is not as difficult as I thought it would be. I relate it to being a handyman. Just as it is enjoyable for a man to fix and repair homes and machines, so it is for a writer to revise a book with the same feeling of retuning. I have traveled so far in my first writing trip that I have the perseverance to reach my destination. With so much work achieved and writing skills developing, to quit this project at this point is not an option. A published book is imminent.

I have learned that you must prepare your mind for whatever you set out to accomplish. We must make our minds a steel trap in which no negative thought-robbing person can enter. We must write down our thoughts so we can see them. If we can see what is in our minds by a written plan through thought, we can begin to take actions steps. No one knows what you want better than you do, and once you publicly announce your creative vision, so-called reality experts will freely offer their opinion on your ambitious plan and the reason why it won't work. If I have an idea that's not working, I want to hear solutions that will make it work. But it seems the population of discouraging people outnumbers the population of encouraging people. God knows your dream because He gave it to you, so I would highly suggest seeking His advice in prayer, and with patience and a heart for God, His answer will come to you. There are people who want to give a person with a dream their opinionated counseling, and perhaps it is in sincerity to protect that person from failure. People who are creative and resourceful are not failures. Maybe you had a great idea at a bad time. Maybe you had a dream or ambition to achieve something in life and no one supported you or cheered you on. People are fallible. That's why I'm so reliant on the Lord, who is infallible.

I was listening to an audio program by Zig Ziglar who

declared (and I'm paraphrasing) that his wife cheering him on to personal success and victory fueled his perseverance. Jean Ziglar supported her husband and stood by him in lean times and prosperous periods. With her love and belief in her husband, he marched on toward victory, and this dynamic husband-and-wife team reaped the fruits of their labor together as a family.

During the writing of this book, I worked on this as a single, divorced dad not having the support of a loving and believing wife. If not for my Lord and Savior and the determination to be a winner for my daughter, I would have quit this project long ago.

Failure means changing plans, not quitting the project. We defeat failure by being persistent in our goals, and we are determined to reach them. Trying and failing is not the problem; failing and quitting is. Failure is a part of life, and it builds that persevering character in us to strive for success and victory. You're not a failure if you attempt at achieving a goal and missing the target. You must restructure your plan and aim for the bull's-eye.

Failure does not indicate lack of intelligence. I believe failure is a way to test us if that goal in our lives is really what we desire. A difficult goal builds perseverance and determination in a person. If achieving our goals were easy, would we appreciate our success? If we want something that is good for us and benefits humanity, then failure is only a wall we have to break down. You must make your plans and set your goals. Without goals and deadlines, your dream will not get off the ground. Fear can hold us back from succeeding in our goals. What we really fear is what people will say when we try and fail.

I pray in everything I do. I have set some goals in my life before and failed. Looking back in retrospect, I now realize I was aiming at the wrong targets. As far as what people think, I only focus on what God thinks. God does not change. He only wants us His creations to glorify Him in our talents He gave us. People change minute by minute so I can't please them, but I know I please Him by glorifying God in everything I do in my life. When you focus on God, life becomes easier. Speaking to all inventive and creative people when you make a mistake, you are in good company. Many great inventors made numerous errors before their dream discoveries became a working reality.

A teacher once told one of these inventors that he was a dreamer and wouldn't amount to anything in life, but he didn't give up, and today, his creativity has lit our world and provided jobs. Thomas Edison is an inspiration. I believe many resourceful people are not pursuing their ideas and ambitions because a despairing message permeated their mind from someone who lives in a gloomy, miserable world and rebels against possibilities.

Innovative people search for solutions to problems. They don't believe in "can't do" thinking. They work on "can do" problem solving. Our creativity brightens a gloomy world. Our ideas need tuning up to improve them so they can take flight. So many ideas and talents are locked up in the minds of numerous individuals just waiting to be born. Some great inventions are waiting to be discovered. A great story is waiting to be written. A wonder song is waiting to be composed. An instrument is waiting to play beautiful music. An inspiring movie is waiting to be produced. But without inspiration and belief that fuels personal initiative to bring these ambitions to life, the dream, the idea, will go to the grave with the mind it came from. Don't let that happen to you!

What do you want to do? Start a business? Take dance

lessons? Become a doctor and heal people? Or become a lawyer and protect a person's American right to freedom? Whatever talent or resource that is within you, it is okay to ask advice of other people, but remember, you are the one living your life, not other people. It is okay to take someone's counsel, but let your final decision be yours. Counsel shouldn't be control.

Do you have a story in you that will inspire someone or entertain him or her while he or she reads and passes the time in a waiting room? Maybe you told bedtime stories to your children. Did you write them down? It's not too late to start right now. First, you must think about what you like to spend your spare time doing, and if it becomes lucrative for you, it can turn into a full-time passion of yours. Whatever you choose to do in life, you must have a passion for it. Otherwise, you are doing something you despise doing. Pray on it. Any idea or thought we have comes from our mind, and because God created our bodies, He is the author of our resources.

A spiritual attack is also aimed at our minds, so we need God's heavenly forces to surround us with love, encouragement, and inspiration. Does that surprise you that God is for your dreams and ideas? When you put God in anything you do and give him the glory, anything is possible. God loves you, and He wants to show His love through you the resourceful, creative believer who adores Him.

Avoiding people who carry stinking thinking in their mind is difficult, but remember that you cannot control other people's toxic behaviors. However, you can control your attitude, along with what you allow to enter and be stored in your mind. It is important to protect and prepare our minds with positive, reinforcing mental messages to keep us focused on our objectives toward our goals. For a creative person, it is not a matter of proving people wrong. We know an inventive idea or creative imagination is within us that other people cannot see, and disparaging people fail to see our vision.

I advise you to write down on paper what you desire most to do, whatever your talent or idea is. You cannot take action if your idea stays in your mind. When you write down your thoughts on paper, they become physical, and you begin to see them. Your intangible thought can now be established into a tangible written plan. If you see the written thought, you believe it. Then you can turn it into a workable plan once you take well-thought-out action steps.

Belief is the key ingredient of "You believe it; you can achieve it." I always carry a notepad with me, for I never know when a thought may enter my mind. I also understand the importance of a written plan that works toward the goal to be achieved. I have a written plan as a writer. Once I saw my ideas and thoughts on paper, my hope grew that, with perseverance and determination, this goal would become reality. You need a written plan with a goal and a deadline; otherwise, you may become a procrastinator like I used to be.

I have been told it takes, on average, about five years to produce your first book. Procrastination can cause it to take longer or not even accomplished at all. I am closing on my fifth year as I write this sentence. However, if you are writing a book, I wouldn't base the timing on mine because this type of book requires extensive research. Maybe you are writing a fiction novel from your own creative imaginary that does not require accurate research.

Once you have your written plan and your goal, set a date to have it finished. You are on your way. You must consistently work on a very important detail, and I mention this quite often.

Perhaps this advice may get repetitious, but it only takes a ten-cent nail in a tire to stop a luxurious Cadillac. The Cadillac is symbolic to your dream and enterprising spirit; the nail is symbolic to that negative toxic person who has free advice on why you should quit your aspirations.

Once you have established your plan and begin to work on the goals you set out to achieve, the only obstacles that can stop you are the toxic messages you allow to take residence in your mind. We talk to people every day and receive mental messages, whether we realize it or not. Some people can be very suggestive and influencing in their spoken word, and depending on how they use it, they can build your confidence or destroy it. It is not called the power of suggestion for nothing. When someone speaks to us, his or her words are powerful. And because these words and suggestions can influence our thinking, we have to determine if it is delivered in a constructive or destructive nature. The words we speak have power, and they can have a tremendous effect in other people's lives depending on what that individual's outlook on life is. Our speech can be very influential and mentally suggestive, and if spoken carelessly, it can cause a great deal of harm. We have the ability to verbally build our friends and loved ones to greatness or mentally destroy their character and goals with toxic spoken expression.

Have you ever had days when you were talking to someone and the wrong words came out? Imagine if we had an instant rewind button that withdrew our harsh words before they reached the ears and minds of our listeners. Well, we don't have a delete button on our ill thoughts, but we do have the ability to think before we speak. We can ask ourselves, "Does the question hinder or help? Will my words help someone positively or negatively?"

It is important to condition our minds and protect our ideas from toxic people who want to share their stinking thinking with anyone who will listen. Only a professional can explain why certain people feel it is their duty in life to dampen or dissolve our enthusiasm toward our pursuits and achievements. Our aspirations are that helium-filled balloon that has been let loose. Because it is fragile in its structure, any sharp object can puncture it and destroy it. The same goes for our dreams and aspirations when the stinging, barbed words from a disparaging and gloomy person can destroy our ambitious, innovative spirit. Don't let dream stealers or any toxic person get in your mind. Don't drain your energy trying to figure out why toxic people do what they do. Your responsibility is to focus your energy on your creativity and resourcefulness.

I highly recommend books and audio material on professional motivational speakers. They are extremely helpful in maintaining positive focus and encouragement when you can't get that from people around you. Listening to speakers of inspiration, along with reading the Word of God, is extremely effective, for, ultimately, the Bible is the original book written and established for inspiration and hope. In the process of writing this book, I continued my course in composition improvement with my daughter and my Lord cheering me on.

Just like a sports team needs its fans and a cheering squad, so do we who have a goal to pursue need to be cheered on to the finish line. My cheering squad consisted of my daughter who is learning to put her thoughts and ideas on paper. Further inspiration in my life comes from listening to Christian radio where I hear music and life lessons where people are blessed and glorify God in praise. The Internet has also provided reliable people of faith through uplifting words and videos. I also received inspiring messages through my pastor's Sunday life lessons in church. I am blessed that I have not had writer's block. I keep a pocket notepad wherever I go, and when I'm busy in my daily work and family responsibilities, valuable thoughts will flood my mind, and I quickly write them down. Some of my co-workers have observed me writing in my pad and have often commented, "Make sure you get my name right," or they'll say, "Leave my name out."

I always directed my thoughts to the book. I have even pulled my truck over to the side of the road many times because a great idea to write about in this book and my other writing projects would fill my mind. On occasion, I would have to explain to the person expecting my arrival why I was late. Honestly, I have never been that late from writing a little note. Probably my party's time clock was too fast. My ideas and subjects that I wanted to write about have abounded without obstacles, so I haven't had to combat writer's block so far as I knock on the wood table I'm writing on right now.

I have kept forging on when I'm by myself and no one is available to cheer me on. I keep pictures of my daughter around me, and I have some plaques of spiritual and inspirational nature to keep me going strong. Actually, only a few people knew I was working on a writing project because I happened to mention it when they asked what was new in my life. Other than a few people, I kept my project and my aspirations to be a writer to myself. I thought that, if I hinted anything about writing a book, some people might think it was just another phase I was going through, like an adult looking for another gig to make money or a person so bored with life that he searched for another hobby.

People in general tend to have stereotypes in their minds.

It isn't their fault. That's just how we human beings are. When you are seen performing one task or job and you do it well, people generally out of habit hold you to that position. It is like taking a mental picture of you, and that is the only photo they have. No other mental portraits of you doing something else are in their mind. Perhaps they never saw you doing any other work. Because of this mental tunnel vision, the ability to provide inspiration to pursue something better seldom follows. I considered myself a prospective writer, and I saw a published book imminent. I did not see my days as the same old stuff.

I became focused on my goals, and my passion for writing has been fueled. Every day has brought new and fresh ideas flowing into my mind, brewing with great faith and excitement. The ideas and thoughts on what to write about were always there because I put them there.

I tried this mind exercise, and it works. Our subconscious mind will work for us if we give it instruction. I found a quiet place and then asked myself, "What can I write about?"

I meditated on this question for a few minutes. After that, I went about my business with a pad and pen in my pocket, ready for use at any time. If I were to sit down and stare at a blank sheet of paper, nothing would come to my mind. Our subconscious mind does not work on our time, but it does labor. This part of our mind works when it is ready, no matter where we are or what we are doing. Whether we work by day or sleep by night, our subconscious will have an answer. That's why it's important to be ready to write down these flashes of thought and creativity on paper. I have used this exercise often, and it works. We can't force ideas. We have to let them happen.

My problems were in the time schedule and energy department of my life, figuring out where to put writing time without taking time away spent with my loved ones. During this time, I ruled out getting back into active service with the volunteer fire department in my area, at least until this first book is finished and published. On numerous days, I would come from work exhausted. I am responsible to my boss in reporting the work progress of the machine I operate. I also have two evenings a week traveling back and forth to get my daughter for my visitation, which I spend with her working on homework during school days. We spend summer days with outside activities as much as possible. When a dad sacrifices his time and weariness after a day at work for his child's playtime and learning time, he is rewarded. For this dad to hear "Daddy, you're the greatest" I can only imagine how much joy God must feel when His children tell Him that He is the greatest!

I am also a responsible son taking over what my dad used to do until he passed away, bringing my mother to her appointments and making sure she is getting proper care. I am also there for companionship, taking her out to an occasional movie. There are days when I have no ambition to write due to the responsibilities of the day of being a responsible employee, son, and dad, exhausting my time and energy. (The time spent with my daughter is pure joy.) I have taken advantage of every spare moment to write. I also had every other weekend to myself, although I would use a weekend to get my mother out of her house for the day. (It is a shame that parents and grandparents are getting left behind. I wasn't raised that way.)

My daughter has caught my enthusiasm for writing, which has sparked her creativity. I give her my utmost support to follow her dream, whether it is to be a writer or to follow any other purpose in life she longs to fulfill in her life. No matter what naysayer or disparaging person may tell her, my counsel to her is, as long as she gives glory to God, her ambitions will be rewarded. By cheering her on, it helps me to stay focused on my goals.

I receive further inspiration to continue my writing aspirations in my most difficult and discouraging days through Christian radio and my pastor's messages at church. That is one major reason I never stayed away from that small chapel I now call my home. When the world knocks me down, I know the pastor can spiritually reenergize me.

The messages of Tony, from whom I believe the Lord works through, always speak to me, and I can hear God's voice through these life-changing and inspiring words not to give up! Although this book is an account of my spiritual walk, I am inspired to continue my other writing projects in fiction. One of them will be a look into the lives of extraordinary neighborhood citizens of a suburban community who serve their neighbors in distress without hesitance or regret as volunteer firefighters and ambulance squad members.

I believe God gave me this gift to be able to express myself and entertain through the written word. However, if my friend Lisa Hartley had not acknowledged my ability to write with eloquence, my ideas and dreams would still be locked up in my mind, never to be a source of encouragement and entertainment to another person in need. The encouragement you can give to someone is monumental. Sometimes, I will be discussing the importance of encouragement, and I'll hear someone react with, "Well, no one ever gave me encouragement!"

When I hear a person answer with those emotionally charged words, it grieves me, and because of this, I am so conscious of the words I speak to others. Many adults have that inner child who never received a kind or inspiring word.

Parents and schoolteachers are in the best position for inspiration and encouragement. They are the most influential role models for a child's creative development. Yet the opportunity for a dream to come true is denied due to lack of vision to see the potential in a child. Maybe you were told that you are a dreamer and you need to leave la-la land. The technology we have today was the idea of a person who dared to dream in his or her yesterday.

Numerous movies have been made from someone's imagination. I recently watched a dated interview with an acclaimed producer/director who was called a daydreamer in school. A famous inventor was told he wouldn't amount to anything. We are not the experts on other people's dreams, so we need to be careful. Our reality is not everyone's truth. Many great resourceful people of our time pushed until their ideas became reality, and I'm sure a naysayer told many of them to give up.

In order to pursue your ambition, you must believe in it, and it must benefit humanity. All things are possible through Christ who strengthens us. God's Word gives us hope and promise that all things are possible through Him. We have to keep our hearts open and available to God. People can be very critical at times, especially the people you love. If you have critical people in your life, don't try to change them. Instead, change your attitude toward them. Pray that God will bless you with loving, inspiring people who want to see you succeed in your quest. You may need to reprogram your mind with positive messages and erase those toxic messages that were placed in your mind from the past if you are going to succeed in your future.

One problem hindered me from my youth, and it stayed with me until one day when I erased it from my mind by taking action. Are you carrying a word of mockery in your mind from your past? Maybe a derogatory nickname that classmates called you in school? Many of us remember that old school adage, "Sticks and stones may break my bones, but names will never hurt me," from childhood. What a lie! You can heal from physical pain. In fact, some young lads show off their scars as badges of courage. But names of mockery leave a painful mental scar in our minds that never go away. We have the power to change this condition. I believe mockery is a sick form of mental abuse and power. When someone calls you a derogatory name and he or she sees that it bothers you, your reaction of annoyance may give that person a twisted sense of power.

In school, I had many mock names due to my body size. I was very thin and undersized, and I didn't grow into physical maturity until later in my teens. My mother has a picture of me in my marching uniform with my father in his uniform on my right and my maternal grandfather on my left when Dad and I marched in the fire department parades. I was sixteen in that picture, but age wise, I looked like I was twelve.

I recall a television show back in the 1970s about high school teenagers in the 1950s. My older sister used to watch it, so occasionally I would watch it with her. From my perspective, this show made high school seem really cool, and I couldn't wait to get to my high school years. Boy, was I in for a surprise. I started wearing glasses when I was nine years old. I grew up in a middle-class working family. We were neither wealthy nor dirt poor. My parents provided the needs for my siblings and me. Unfortunately, our society always has exceedingly high standards that families constantly struggle to keep up with. I didn't wear the up-to-date fashion shirts and jeans that my other male classmates sported with their teen egos, but I wasn't dressed in rags either. My attire also consisted of these oval-rimmed glasses that made me look bug-eyed. My legs were like bones wrapped in skin. My thin frame consisted of very little muscle tissue. I was one of those unfortunate souls who had a "kick me" sign stuck to my back while walking to my next class. I was shy and very timid. Television, although it is considered entertainment, has influence in our everyday lives, and this particular show made high school appear like the place to be for hip and cool teenagers. Not so when you are a late-blooming teenager wearing dark-rimmed spectacles and carrying an underweight body that a stiff wind could blow over.

I had many mock names in school, and I was a prime target for the school bully. (Bullies never pick on someone their own size.) I struggled with ways to improve my weight and body structure, but I would need proper guidance and instruction on weightlifting, which wasn't offered to me at that time. When I entered junior high school, we were given a tour of the weight-lifting room. I remember that day crystal clear when I sat down at the Nautilus machine and lifting a weight that was very light, but I could feel the power and potential in that brief lift. Oh, the possibilities I could have if I could just get a weight training program in school. When I asked my gym teacher about using the weight room, he peered over his bifocals down at me.

Before he spoke, his body language was already speaking through his long, doubt-ridden face as he grimly stated, "Mr. Lown, that is not part of your curriculum."

My hope of having a healthier muscular physique was crushed that day with those words, and I became a student who only wanted to do enough work to graduate and get out of that place. I did graduate high school, although I had to take two summer school classes in order to get my diploma. One of those classes was physical education. That summer was agonizing.

There is some irony and encouragement here. I continued to struggle with my frail, bony body and desperately wanted to have some natural muscle mass until January 1, 1993. Just before my twenty-seventh birthday, a co-worker suggested I try a gym that had just opened about a half hour from our workplace. In my mind, I linked a public gym to the same situation as my high school gym experience where I was not encouraged. They'd probably mock me in a public gym, just as they did in high school. I finally gathered the gumption to enter that gym, and when I was given a tour of this gym, many of the members working out stared at me, but it wasn't a gaze of intimidation or mockery. They knew just by looking at me why I walked through those doors, and it was the best decision I ever made. My next best decision would be accepting Christ seven years later. I learned the big difference between a public gym and a school gym where I received the coaching and guidance I needed and achieved the results I so longed for. I had started a training program that first week when a bodybuilder walked up to me as I was watching his partner bench-press a bar weight of two hundred and fifty pounds. His words of inspiration are still in my head.

"You might not lift this today, and you might not lift it next month or next year, but if you focus and never give up, one day soon, you will lift that much weight."

Hope was born that day, and the public gym became my best friend where I could finally build my confidence and esteem. Incidentally four years later, under the careful watch of a reliable spotter, I benched two hundred and fifty pounds with one repetition while maintaining a natural diet. Whatever you aspire to do in your life, don't give up!

We often equate dreams to being financially set in life and

doing things we want to do. Not all dreams and ambitions are about piles of money surrounding us. Sometimes, money dreams that come true without a life of purpose can turn into a personal nightmare because money feeds our self-centeredness. I gave this deep thought about my own pursuits and ambitions. Did they come true? Every dream needs inspiration. When I was sixteen, my father and cousins inspired me to join our volunteer fire department. I was also encouraged to be the best firefighter I could be. I aspired to become fire chief, and although that did not come to pass, I was elected first lieutenant fire officer. Everything I did in the volunteer fire service, I gave 110 percent. I resigned in 2002 when my daughter was born because of the fact that I give so much I did not want to deprive my daughter of precious time together, not knowing the divorce would occur six years later. Divorced dads get limited time with their children as it is. I have learned the most precious gift I can give my daughter is my undivided time and attention, and the benefits of being a hero to your own child are priceless.

Another ambition I had was to ride a street bike, but I didn't own a bike or have a license to ride. Shortly after my twenty-ninth birthday, my cousin gave me his older bike. The motor was in pieces. He told me, if I bought the part it needed and put it back together, the bike would be mine. It was the opportunity I needed not only to own my first motorcycle but also to learn motorcycle mechanics. With the help of my friend (the same one I raced pickup trucks with) who had the mechanical know-how and tools we needed, we put the bike back together and running like clockwork. That was a dream come true since I first took it to a bike repair shop and the head mechanic told me the bike was a basket case with no hope of putting that heap back together.

My old friend and workplace mentor, Jimmy Higgs, another inspirational person in my life, went out riding with me while I learned for the first time to ride a street bike. He followed me in his own pickup truck to the testing area where I passed my motorcycle test.

As an employee of the highway department, my boss, Dennis Miller, has always acknowledged my determined work ethics to get the job done, and I have received words of encouragement from him. I couldn't ask for a better and forgiving employer.

I longed to be a father although I had doubts about this dream because I was married before and never had children. At the age of thirty-six in my second marriage, it was official. I became not just a father, but an involved and active dad. I had prayed to God, whom I now have a relationship with, that I would be given the privilege of having a child of my own loins in my second marriage. In my first marriage, I did not know God personally; nor did I have Christ as my Savior. Not all of these desired ambitions might seem like a big dream like fortune or fame, but if you are not doing what you love or were born to do, then it is a dream never to be lived.

This book is a dream, and I asked myself why I wanted to write a book like this. I wanted to help someone who may have experienced some of the trials of life I have gone through. I also hope to give hope and inspiration to those who need encouragement through faith. My faith is a continual learning process that has taught me redemption forgiveness. That is the love of God. My faith has brought me truth through the Bible. What I have learned in my walk, I want to share with other believers who may have experienced trials in their own lives and encourage them to maintain their walk with God. Maybe you have had a less than friendly experience with someone who called himself or herself a Christian. Believers are Christians by their acts of love. The only person who is perfect in our faith is our leader, Jesus Christ. We who are not perfect follow Him who is perfect. When we understand that all people are fallible and we will be let down at some point, it is less of a shock, and that is what the Bible reveals.

Before I received Christ, I didn't think anyone would lie to me. How many times was I let down when I realized he or she did? I am now assured that, even though people will let me down, I won't stay down for Christ will lift me to my feet. Those who choose to live for Christ are not perfect. We will fall because of our fallen nature.

Earlier, I discussed the issue of mockery and names and my school experiences of being bullied. Those mock names I was given in school don't bother me anymore because I'm not the same person. When I received Christ as my Savior, I became a new creation. The most inspiring messages I have found for reassurance in my life is in church when I hear God's message through my pastor. If God is for me, who can be against me? No one is greater than my God. He is bigger than any fear. The Bible is inspirational, and to read it is to know who God is and what He wants for your life. He gave us a purpose in life that He is waiting for us to claim! He created us with the ability to dream through our imagination and creativity. He wants us to use the talents He gave us. He wants us to humbly pursue our ambitions and share our blessings with others. God is glorified when we reach our goals and share our love for other people. The only way people will know God's love is through those who carry His love in their heart. Our creative resourcefulness is a sign of God's love to all of His children who know Him.

Chapter 8

Message of Salvation

Everyone loves getting something for free. We walk into a store, and when we hear them announce a free giveaway of some sort, we dash to the line. Some people have a motto, "If it's for free, it's for me." Yes, we all love free things with no strings attached. Something that is free is considered a gift, and we are surprised. Here's a surprise. God offers something for free. God offers us eternal salvation, a free gift through Jesus Christ. God made personal salvation so simple with no tricks involved. All we have to do is confess our sins to God and believe His only Son died on the cross for us and was resurrected from the dead. Now Jesus the Messiah sits on the right side of the Father. Jesus did all we could not do. All we have to do is confess, receive, and believe. God is great! Once we receive Christ as our Savior, our personal transformation begins instantly within us to prepare us for our new home in heaven, living forever in the presence of God, our loving Father, surrounded by His glory, love, and light.

What God gains through our salvation is an unspotted relationship with the ones He created. We all have fallen natures because of the sin that is in our lives, but God created us. And despite our sinful nature, He loves His creation.

I want to share with you what it means to receive Christ. If only my heart were open to this message in my youth. Would my life be different if I had accepted Jesus at an early age? Yes, I absolutely believe it would be. I received Christ as my Savior just before my thirty-fourth birthday. I know I cannot change my past, but I also know I have a brighter and hopeful future. I have been transformed into a new creation, and it is through Christ that all things are possible for me.

Pastor Lou counseled me that my life may become difficult because of the changes that the Lord will do in my heart. I will no longer do the things I used to do that displease Him and cause harm to me. He will give me a spiritual heart like His. What breaks the Lord's heart now breaks mine. Pastor Lou shared with me that worldly thinking would not accept these changes I allow the Lord to make in my heart; nor those who like the old me would accept my lifestyle. He added that, because I want to do things that please God, many people in my life who don't have this heavenly understanding may keep a distance from me.

I do not regret becoming a believer in Christ and living for Him. I'm very confident in my faith. I'm not the same self-serving man I was, for I have chosen to be a servant of the Lord and not to be served like my former self. The trials I have faced are not because God is against me. No, these trials have tested my spiritual mettle perhaps to see if I will walk away from faith under conflict. I came very close to walking away from faith when the divorce hit me. I couldn't understand why everyone seemed to walk away from me when I accepted Christ. In my old religion, everyone loved me, and I did good works. But God showed me how He transformed me in that I'm sober and clean of lustful media and I'm reverent to God in my verbal language. I believe I went through these trials because everyone was watching me to see if I would walk away and try something else. But faith isn't something you try for a while. It is a relationship with Jesus Christ. This faith I have chosen is real, and I have seen God's fingerprints in my life. God's Holy Spirit resides in my heart. I want to please God in all areas of my life. When I'm called home, I have the confidence that I will be with my heavenly Father and my Savior who took my place on that cross.

You, too, can have that confidence. Would you like to receive the gift of eternal life? This is very important matter, so let's clarify what it involves. You need to do the following:

- Transfer your trust from what you have been doing to what Christ has done for you on His cross.
- Accept Christ as your personal savior. Open the door to your heart and invite Him in. He says, "Behold, I stand at the door and knock; if any man hear my voice, and open the door, I will come in to him" (Rev. 3:20).
- Receive Jesus Christ as Lord. Give Him the driver's seat and controls to your life.
- Repent. Be willing to turn from anything that is not pleasing to Him. He will reveal His will to you as you grow in your relationship with Him.

Now if this is really what you want, you can go to God in prayer. Right where you are, you can receive His gift of eternal life through Jesus Christ right now. "For in your heart that you believe and are justified, and it is with your mouth that you confess and are saved" (Rom. 10:10). If you want to receive the gift of eternal life through Jesus Christ, then call on Him, asking Him for this gift right now.

Here is a prayer for you to pray right now.

> *Lord Jesus Christ, I confess I'm a sinner and do not deserve eternal life. But I believe you died for me and you rose from the grave to purchase a place in heaven for me. Lord Jesus, come into my life, take control of my life, forgive me of my sins, and save me. I repent of my sins and now place my trust in You for my salvation. I accept the free gift of eternal life through Jesus Christ.*

If this prayer is the sincere desire of your heart, look at what Jesus promises to those who believe in Him. "I tell you the truth, he who believes has everlasting life" (John 6:47). Once you have prayed this prayer, you may be wondering what you do next. The answer is nothing other than allowing the Lord to reside in your heart and your life. He will make wonderful changes in your life. You are now a new creation. When you were first born, you were born of the flesh. Once you receive Christ as you Savior, you are born again of the spirit of Christ. You no longer live for your pleasure, but you live for Christ, along with pleasing God. I encourage you to read through the Bible and pray for understanding if you don't comprehend the words. The Bible is God's way of living. Because we lived the way of the world, the Bible may appear foreign to us in that it glorifies God, but I encourage you to persevere in your quest to know and draw closer to the God who created you, wants a relationship with you, and has great plans for you!